Stand
by YOUR
TRUTH

Stand by Your TRUTH

RICKEY SMILEY

WITH CHARISSE JONES

GALLERY BOOKS

New York   London   Toronto   Sydney   New Delhi

G

Gallery Books
An Imprint of Simon & Schuster, Inc.
1230 Avenue of the Americas
New York, NY 10020

First Gallery Books trade paperback edition October 2018

GALLERY BOOKS and colophon are registered trademarks of Simon & Schuster, Inc.

For information about special discounts for bulk purchases,
please contact Simon & Schuster Special Sales at 1-866-506-1949
or business@simonandschuster.com.

The Simon & Schuster Speakers Bureau can bring authors to your live event.
For more information or to book an event, contact the Simon & Schuster Speakers Bureau at 1-866-248-3049 or visit our website at www.simonspeakers.com.

Interior design by Davina Mock-Maniscalco

Manufactured in the United States of America

10   9   8   7   6   5   4   3   2   1

The Library of Congress has cataloged the hardcover edition as follows:

Names: Smiley, Rickey author. | Jones, Charisse author.
Title: Stand by your truth : and then run for your life! / Rickey Smiley with Charisse Jones.
Description: New York : Gallery Books, 2017.
Identifiers: LCCN 2017033485 | ISBN 9781501178603 (hardback) | ISBN 9781501178610 (trade paperback)
Subjects: LCSH: Smiley, Rickey. | Comedians—United States—Biography. | Conduct of life—Humor. | BISAC: BIOGRAPHY & AUTOBIOGRAPHY / Personal Memoirs. | BIOGRAPHY & AUTOBIOGRAPHY / Rich & Famous. | HUMOR / Form / Essays.
Classification: LCC PN2287.S565 A3 2017 | DDC 792.702/8092 [B] —dc23
LC record available at https://lccn.loc.gov/2017033485

ISBN 978-1-5011-7860-3
ISBN 978-1-5011-7861-0 (pbk)
ISBN 978-1-5011-7862-7 (ebook)

CONTENTS

TO THE PARENTS

Being a father is the most rewarding thing in the world. But it's also hard work that can disappoint you and bring you down lower than just about anything else. It hurts to not be appreciated, and it hurts to be disrespected. Don't think for a minute that just because I'm on the radio, and my family and I have a popular TV show, we don't go through challenges. For every situation that we neatly resolve on the air, there are a dozen more that we have to deal with when the cameras aren't around.

Right now, my house is quiet. But just last year, I was trying to keep it all together dealing with my four children. There was my younger biological son, Malik, who's now fifteen. His mother, Elizabeth, already had a young daughter, D'essence, when we began dating. By the time our relationship ended, D'essence basically considered me her father, and I have lovingly claimed her as my daughter ever since. She's now nineteen.

Aaryn was two years old when she came into my world. I had a relationship with her mother, and we continued to co-parent Aaryn even after we broke up. She's the same age as Malik, so I've always referred to the two of them as my twins, and Aaryn has spent pretty much every weekend, holiday, and summer of her childhood staying with me.

And then there is Brandon, who at twenty-six is my oldest child, and other biological son. I was in college, and his mom, Nicole, was in high school, when he was born. I went to court to win custody of Brandon and the battle took years, but I was determined to be there for him, just as I was there for Malik and for D'essence and for Aaryn, though I broke up with their mothers long ago.

Those are just the kids who are *technically* mine. I've also been a father figure to several young men whom I call my nephews, though they are not related to me biologically. My nephew Craig has called my house home. And though they never officially lived with me, I've helped raise my best friend T. West's two sons, T. J. and Terrell, since T. was tragically murdered a decade ago, as well as a whole lot of other young people whom I have tried to mentor and guide over the years.

I understood from an early age the importance of doing all that you can for the next generation, including young people with whom you might not share a drop of blood. I saw that example set by members of my extended family, and it was reinforced again and again by the community of coaches, employers, and mentors who helped me find my way through every stage of my life.

My grandfather Ernest Smiley Sr. taught me what it means to be a generous, hardworking man. I started working for him when I was nine or ten years old, earning five dollars a week mowing lawns and trimming shrubs. He spent his weekdays at a local steel plant, and he also owned a landscaping business that he operated on the weekends. Then there were the men who led my peewee football team, Coach Ausley, Coach Henderson, and Coach Holmes. They toughened me up by teaching me to hit back, and they showed me how to focus on a goal and not to give up until I'd achieved it.

I carried those lessons about hard work and determination with me when I went off to college. It wasn't long before I was able to put them to use, when my good friend Charles "Chucky" Jenkins gave me a referral that would change the course of my life.

One night, Chucky and I went to the Comedy Club. It was one of the most famous comedy venues in the country and Chucky, an up-and-coming comedian, was the opening act for a comic named Trip Winfield. I took a seat out in the audience and ordered a Coke, and as I watched Chucky spin stories under the spotlight, a thought ran through my mind—"Man, I can do this."

I knew I was funny. My friends and I would get together, in a dining hall on campus or on the side of the dance floor at a fraternity party, and we would crack "yo mama" jokes until our stomachs hurt from laughing so hard. I had also grown up around some great joke-tellers. When my grandparents started teasing each other, especially after they had a couple of cocktails on a Saturday night, they were as funny as Redd Foxx and LaWanda Page on *Sanford and Son*. I knew that performing at a comedy club would require a different level of joking around, but I wanted to try.

When I mentioned my idea to Chucky, he told me that the Comedy Club had an open mic night every Tuesday. He encouraged me to call the club's owner, Bruce Ayers, and tell him Chucky had referred me.

A few days later, I was standing backstage with six or seven other amateur comedians, learning the house rules from Bruce. "You've got five minutes," Bruce said. "And keep your act clean."

It was November 13, 1989, and half an hour later, I was cracking jokes on the stage for the first time.

My act was so-so. I managed to squeeze a few laughs out of the two dozen people who were sitting in the audience. But even in front

of such a small crowd, I felt a ripple of excitement standing there at the mic. I liked the challenge of getting the guy who was sweet-talking his girlfriend in the middle of my routine to stop whispering in her ear and listen to my jokes. I wanted to come back and try again the following Tuesday, and Bruce told me that would be okay.

From then on, I was at the Comedy Club every week. Bruce encouraged me, allowing me to keep polishing my act. My observations were getting sharper, and my lines were getting stronger. I started feeling more comfortable, and I began to improvise jokes onstage instead of sticking to a tight script. I didn't notice too many audience members chatting through my act anymore. They were paying attention to what was happening on the stage, having a good time, and laughing.

One night, about four months later, Bruce asked to see me in his office. That felt like the longest walk of my life. I had butterflies in my stomach, worrying that he was going to tell me not to come back to the club. I racked my brain. "Did I accidentally curse? Did people tell him to pull that not-funny, weak-joke-telling fool off of the stage?"

As it turned out, Bruce's wife had been in the audience that evening. She thought I was so funny that she ran backstage to tell Bruce to come out and watch my routine. After he saw me perform, and he heard the crowd's reaction to my act, Bruce made a decision. He wanted to hire me as a permanent opening act, providing the lead-in to the headliners who appeared at the club on Saturday nights. I wouldn't be the only one in that slot, so it wouldn't happen every week, but I could count on that gig at least once every other month. And I would be paid one hundred dollars for every eight shows.

I know that wasn't much money, but I couldn't believe that I was going to get paid at all to do stand-up comedy. After I accepted his offer, I walked to my car with tears in my eyes. That was the beginning

of my warming up the crowd for great comics like George Wallace, Rita Rudner, and finally, one night, Steve Harvey.

I was young, still finding my way, but Bruce's willingness to take a chance on me, to give me an opportunity to polish my craft and grow, helped me to create my future. So I take nurturing and encouraging young people very seriously. And we should start first with those growing up inside our own homes.

I know that I am a good father. I am there for my children, regardless of whether the situation is good or bad. I've changed diapers and warmed up baby formula. I took Malik to the emergency room when his fever wouldn't break, and I sat there worrying and waiting until the doctors said that it was safe to take him home. I've attended parent-teacher conferences and told my kids afterward how proud I was when the reports were good, or cracked down when I found out they weren't living up to their academic potential.

And I've been there for the fun stuff, too. I've taken my children to every theme park in the country—Six Flags Great Adventure, Disney World, Universal Studios. We ride bikes and jump on the trampoline together. We've even sailed across the ocean to the Bahamas—not on a cruise ship or a chartered vessel, but on *my* boat, one that I owned *and* captained.

Those are just some of the experiences that I have shared with my children. And they've never even offered to cook me dinner (LOL).

I'm not saying that I do for them expecting something in return. I'm the father, and my actions flow from feelings of affection and a sense of profound responsibility. But a "Happy birthday" would be nice to hear. And I wouldn't mind an invitation every now and then to go with my kids to the movies or a concert, not because they want me to pay, but because they want to spend a little extra time with me.

Father's Day has been a particular disappointment. When it

comes around, my children treat it as though it's just a regular day. On Mother's Day, the world stops. The celebrations start on Thursday and build up over the next three days. The kids trip over themselves getting their mothers flowers, perfume, makeovers, or massages. But Father's Day? It's like comparing Columbus Day to Christmas. I don't necessarily think that kids appreciate their fathers less. But I think society has sent the message, with its television commercials, online ads, and nighttime sitcoms, that outward expressions of affection are meant for Mom, while a nod or a fist bump is good enough for Dad. Still, fathers need love, too, and without the occasional acknowledgment, they can feel taken for granted.

A couple of years ago on Father's Day, my kids showed up an hour late for church. Now, at this point, all of my kids knew how to drive and three of them had their own cars. They didn't have to wait on a bus. They didn't have an excuse to arrive late anywhere, especially church. I let them have it, and they didn't appreciate being scolded.

When we got back home, they walked into the house with a half-melted cake from Dairy Queen. They didn't even *give* it to me. They didn't say, "Happy Father's Day!" or, "We appreciate you!" They just put the cake on the kitchen counter and went upstairs. I threw that soupy mess in the trash.

This past Father's Day was pitiful, too. I got a Build-A-Bear wearing an Alabama Crimson Tide jersey. My kids gave it to me after arriving late at church *again*. Now, I love the Crimson Tide, but at forty-eight years old, I'm way too old for a Build-A-Bear. I'm not asking my kids to buy me an Aston Martin or to get me season tickets to watch the Cleveland Cavaliers play. I have been blessed with more than enough money to buy whatever I want. I just want the occasional gift that shows they put some thought into it and didn't just grab the first thing they could find when they realized that they needed to get me *something*. I love to cook, so how about a cookbook? I'm a classic rock fan, so how about a vintage Christopher Cross record? I love my kids, so how about a framed photo that I didn't take?

Or, even better, how about remembering to take out the garbage without my telling them to do it ten times? Or seeking out a tutor on their own to help get that grade up in trigonometry? Those are gifts that I'd welcome any time of the year. My kids just don't think about the impact of what they do, and how being treated like an afterthought really hurts my feelings.

I've tried hard to teach them to be empathetic. On Christmas Day, we don't sit on the floor unwrapping iPads and PlayStations. Every year, we leave our house at two a.m. with trucks full of toys that we take to twenty to thirty families who don't have anything to wake up to on Christmas morning. We do that until the afternoon and then head back home to get some rest. My children look forward to those excursions every year. I think it makes them feel good to give and not just sit around receiving.

But my kids are sometimes more attuned to the feelings of strangers than they are to those of their own father. It bothers me when they don't remember me on Father's Day or show respect for my efforts to teach them right from wrong. I don't think they understand the worry I feel when they stay out late without calling me, or the concerns I have for their futures when they take a shortcut in school instead of trying to challenge themselves.

I just don't think children in general recognize the kind of pain that they can cause their parents, especially their fathers, whom I believe they expect to be stoic and unflustered. But every time our sons fall and skin their knees, every time our daughters don't get picked by a team they practiced so hard to make, or our children get their hearts broken by a first love, we fathers feel it deeply, too.

I REMEMBER EVERY detail of the day we buried my father. I was seven years old.

I remember my uncles being there. My dad, Ernest Smiley Jr., was the oldest of four brothers. His younger siblings were Eugene, Bandy, and Anthony. Eugene had actually gone to New York City to try to convince my father to come back home to Birmingham, but my father wouldn't do it. A few weeks later, he was dead. I believe that he was stabbed to death, but I don't really know for sure. It was just too painful for my family to talk about at the time, and so the details of what happened are a blur.

We belonged to New St. James Baptist Church, and the pews were packed for my dad's funeral. My grandmother Ada wore a sleeveless white dress with orange and black stripes that stood out against the black outfits my mother, Carolita, my other grandparents, and my uncles wore. My grandmother sat in the row behind my mother, trying to comfort her. But there was no comforting my grandparents. There were not enough hugs, prayers, or psalms in the world to make them feel better.

The day before, the family had held my father's wake, and I remember how nervous my grandfather seemed at the funeral home. He was walking around, looking distracted, and not paying any attention to me. That wasn't like him. He was always so glad when I came into the room, wrapping his arms around my shoulders, making me laugh, or teaching me how to pay bills and remember numbers. So that night, I just couldn't understand why my grandfather wouldn't sit down. I didn't quite get the whole picture until the next day at the funeral. That's when I realized that while I had lost my father, my grandfather had lost a son.

My great-grandparents were there at the funeral, too, sitting in the second row. Mary and Alexander McElroy were the parents of my grandmother Mattie Smiley. Cherry Smiley was the mother of my grandfather Ernest. I remember the choir singing. When a soloist let out the words "Precious Lord, take my hand," both of my grandparents Ernest and Mattie broke down crying, and some of those gathered in the church had to take my grandmother outside. Then it seemed like all of a sudden we were walking out into the daylight. It was April, and the sun was glinting off of two silver Cadillacs that were lined up behind the silver hearse that was going to carry my daddy's casket, covered in a US flag, to the cemetery.

After the burial, when we got back into one of those cars and drove away from the grave, a song by the O'Jays was playing on the radio: "For the Love of Money."

My uncle Anthony was sitting with the US flag that had been draped over my father's casket on his lap. He reached over and turned the radio up a little bit, I guess to lighten the mood. To this day, every time I hear that song, the memories of my father's burial come rushing back.

I didn't see my father that often, so my impressions of him were hazy. But when I got older, and especially after I had my own children, I felt strong emotions about how his life and early, tragic death had affected my grandparents.

My father was living a fast life in New York City. I'm not saying that he was a bad person, but he was associating with a rough crowd. I truly believe that if he had thought more about his parents and how his lifestyle was worrying them, he might have pulled away from those folks and connected with more positive people. I think that he might have made different choices about what he was doing if he had reflected on how his behavior was keeping his mother and father awake at night. How it weighed on their minds during Sunday dinners, on family game nights, and at University of Alabama football games, because they missed him.

His stubbornness and recklessness placed him in dangerous situations, and his death scarred my grandparents for the rest of their lives. They were a hardworking couple who had done all that they could to take care of their children and mold them into productive and God-fearing adults. But after all their efforts and sacrifices, they had to watch their oldest son stray from the values that they had tried to instill in him. And then, one day, they got the call that he was dead.

My father's death affected everyone in our family. At twenty-six years old, he left behind a seven-year-old son, and my mother and all of our relatives had to figure out how to move forward. They had to pick up the baton, fill the void, and, together, help guide me into manhood.

But what really breaks my heart is the thought of my grandparents' grief and the wistful looks that would cross their faces whenever someone in the family mentioned my father's name. That still brings tears to my eyes. I feel their loss more than my own.

And so I truly understand, from my own experiences as well as those of my elders, how challenging and sometimes heartbreaking parenting can be. Not too long ago, I actually sat down with my daughter D'essence. I explained to her how disappointed I sometimes feel when she and her siblings don't bother listening to me, or act as though they don't care about what I do for the family. But at the end of that serious sit-down, I also explained to her that I wouldn't give up being her father for anything.

I applaud all of the grandparents who are out there raising their grandchildren because their sons or daughters are not willing or able to do it. I have nothing but appreciation for the single fathers who are lifting up their kids, despite society's often low expectations of unmarried dads. Also for the mothers who bring children into this world and weather the worries that come with shepherding them through life. I respect all the members of "the village" who don't have a blood connection to the kids down the street, but who choose to love them, look out for them, and motivate them anyway.

Each and every one of us who nurtures, guides, and encourages the next generation is doing the most important work in the world.

TO THE KIDS:
DO THE RIGHT THING

I just want to have a word with the younger generation.

I'm mostly talking about teenagers. Particularly those who are being raised by a single mother or father, a parent who is trying to juggle life's many responsibilities all on their own. Many of you have parents who get up to go to work every day, driving trucks long distances before most people are awake, interacting with customers who show them little respect, or tending to patients who are too weak or ill to express their gratitude. Maybe you have a parent who's running his or her own business, dealing with the stress of managing a team of employees while trying to meet the needs of the customers who stream through the front door.

Your mother or father heads out to greet the world every morning, bright-eyed and full of energy, and returns home in the evening, often looking tired and feeling run-down. Do you ever notice? Do you ever think about what your mom or dad had to deal with in the eight or nine hours between the time they dropped you off at school and told you to have a great day, and the moment they came home, dropped their laptop or purse on a chair, and went into the kitchen to start preparing your dinner? I believe that many of you don't have the slightest idea what your parents go through every day to provide you with those three-hundred-dollar tickets to see Beyoncé in concert, or to buy the electronic fad of the moment that you find under the tree every Christmas. What is even worse, I fear that many of you do not care.

No matter what you are doing or where you are—whether it's sitting in your room watching Netflix, meeting up with friends at Starbucks, or kicking it in the back of the family car—I want you to pull your pants legs up and peer down at the floor. I want you to look at the Steph Curry sneakers that you wanted so badly that are laced around your feet. I want you to think about that Tommy Hilfiger shirt that you're wearing and the Hollister jacket that's draped across your shoulders. Have you ever thought about how much that outfit—which you casually threw on—cost your mom or dad? If someone whipped out a calculator and tallied the price tags for everything you had on from head to toe, it would probably total at least a couple hundred dollars. That's enough money to buy a month's worth of groceries or pay a phone bill, but your parents spent that amount on clothes that made you look and feel good.

I'm guessing that many of you aren't even riding a bus to school. You get dropped off every day by your loving parent, who chauffeurs you to the school's front door. I'll bet that when your mother or father was young, most of them had to walk a long distance, or stand on a chilly corner waiting to board a crowded bus, in order to make it to class on time. But you are able to daydream and send instant messages from the backseat of a warm, cozy car. You are so blessed! Many of you have luxuries that your parents never had.

What I'm asking you to do is to show your parents just a little appreciation, and to not take for granted all that they give you. I want you to make the burden that they carry—working long hours, balancing a household budget, planning your activities—just a little bit lighter. I'd like you to ask your father about his day before he asks you about yours. I want you to make up your bed and put your dirty socks and underwear in the hamper without your mother stomping into your room to demand that you do it. I am asking you to set the table for dinner without being asked, and then to clear and wash the dishes before your mom or dad makes a move toward the kitchen sink. When your parents come back from the supermarket, meet them in the driveway and tote the grocery bags into the house. Let your parents know that you realize what they do for you, and that you value all of it, by showing them gestures of appreciation.

I know that no child asks to be here, and it is a parent's duty to give their children what they need. That's been made clear to me since I was a little boy. I had a mother, two sets of grandparents, and *great*-grandparents who made sure that my sister and I had the nurturing and support that helped us become confident adults who felt committed to our communities. All parents are supposed to instill basic values in their children, as well as provide them with life's necessities. But I believe that anything else parents give—the trips to Disney World, the hoverboards, the pricey sneakers—is all extra, and that their children should recognize how lucky they are to get it.

Your parents are obligated to make sure you eat every day, but they do not owe each of you an iPad. Your parents are responsible for making sure you have a safe space to call home, but they do not owe each of you your own bedroom or an ultra-slim 4K smart TV. Your parents owe you their undivided attention when you tell them about the frustrations you're experiencing with a particular friendship, but they don't owe you a ride to school every morning. They don't owe you their understanding if you aren't making even the tiniest effort to live up to your God-given potential.

I believe that every relationship is a two-way street. Friends owe one another loyalty. The entrepreneur running a café owes her customers good service. The diners owe the restaurant's owner and staff simple, common courtesy and a tab paid in full. And along with love and a whole lot of respect, children owe their parents their strongest effort in whatever they do.

A key place to demonstrate effort is in the classroom. As a young person, schoolwork is probably your primary responsibility, and it's important that you try—and I mean really try—to do your best every day.

When I was in high school, I was a decent student who was able to earn a B in most of my courses without having to stay up all night studying. But in certain subjects, like geometry or Spanish, it was a harder lift for me to earn a top grade.

There were evenings when, after I got home from playing football or grabbing a sandwich at the Waffle House with my friends, the last thing I wanted to do was strain my brain grappling with graphs and grammar. Sometimes, I chose to be lax and just coast along, getting a check minus when I could have earned a check plus on my homework, or getting 75 instead of 100 percent on an exam.

But most of the time, I understood that I needed to put in my strongest effort to do as well as I could, no matter how much I would have preferred listening to my classic rock albums to studying. I believed that I owed that to my mother, Carolita, who worked hard to provide for my sister and me after our father was killed. I owed it to my father's dad, Ernest Sr., who dealt with the monotony of work in a steel plant to make ends meet. And I owed it to my father's mother, Mattie, who worked at the Birmingham international airport. They were proud people, living comfortable, middle-class lives, but they wanted me, my sister, and their other grandchildren to have all the professional options in the world when we grew up and were finally on our own. They emphasized that education was the road map to get us wherever we wanted to go.

When I brought home a strong report card, sprinkled with A's among the B's, my grandfather would stick a few extra dollars in my pocket, while my mother or grandmother would cook me a reward, baking my favorite chocolate-chip cookies or preparing my favorite dinner of smothered chicken, candied yams, and string beans. Even if I didn't get all A's, they appreciated the work I'd put in to do my best.

I don't believe that most parents demand that their children top the honor roll every semester, or that they require their sons and daughters to maintain a 4.0 grade point average year after year. But I *do* think they appreciate knowing that their children are trying to do their best academically. They don't want to see them shrug off what may be the single biggest determinant of their futures.

So all of you who are part of the younger generation need to be diligent with your school assignments. I am a football fanatic, so let me break down what I mean in athletic terms. I want you to feel confident at the end of each semester that you left it all on the field—that you turned in every piece of homework and studied as hard as you possibly could. That's the least you can do for your parents, who do so much for you every day.

And if getting top grades is a struggle, there's something else that every teenager should be able to do, and that is show their parents respect.

Many of us, young and old alike, take the people that we're closest to for granted. The people that we are around each day become so familiar that we can lose sight of how special they are and how much dedication it takes for them to support us in all that we do.

When you're a kid, you probably just assume that you can turn up the temperature on the thermostat, without thinking about the hours your parents put in at work to have the cash to pay the utility bill. You feel confident that your father will drive you to swim class every Saturday, without thinking about how he has to get up early on one of his two days off in order to get you there.

But earning a living and making sure you get wherever you need to go takes a lot of energy. I think that if you stepped back for a moment and really reflected on all the support that you get from your parents—if you thought about all the ordinary, everyday things that they do to make your life comfortable and stable—it would be easier for you to show them the kind of respect they deserve.

For most young people, showing appreciation to their parents is not top-of-mind. As a matter of fact, many teenagers are just plain rude. They're more deferential to the captain of the basketball team or to the makeup artist that they follow on YouTube than they are to their own mothers and fathers.

Some of their rudeness is a by-product of this culture that we live in, where people are so busy clicking and swiping on their tablets and smartphones that they don't know how to look another person in the eye and make a true human connection. A lot of teenagers don't realize that yapping on WhatsApp, Twitter, and Snapchat is no substitute for seeing the expression on a friend's face when you ask them in person how they are feeling.

But some young people are rude because they simply want to be. I see that kind of bad behavior all the time. Not only do some young people fail to voluntarily take out the trash on garbage day or conveniently forget that they need to walk the dog that they begged their parents to buy, but they also talk back whenever their parents ask them to do *anything*.

I remember visiting the home of one of my acquaintances. I

watched his teenage son take what felt like an hour to walk from the living room to the hallway closet, where his dad told him to put away a pair of sneakers that were lying in the middle of the floor. Another evening, I had dinner with a friend's family and when we were finished eating, she asked her daughter to wipe off the table. You would have thought by her funky attitude that my friend had told her to climb into the chimney with a soot broom.

Both kids complained the whole time.

"Why do I have to put the shoes away? They're not mine!"

"Natasha just texted and I have to respond. It's an emergency!"

With all that their parents had on their plates, I couldn't believe that either of those kids had the nerve to talk back. As far as I was concerned, the only things they needed to say were, "Yes, ma'am," "Yes, sir," and "Where is the Windex?" My acquaintance didn't ask who left the shoes in the middle of the floor. He said to put them in the closet where they belonged. And when I looked at my friend's daughter, all I could think was that cleaning the table where she herself had just eaten didn't seem like such an imposition.

I let each of those kids know how I was feeling. I told them that their parents shouldn't have had to ask them to clean up, but once they did, they needed to hurry up and do what they were told. I speak up like that all the time, because I take the responsibility of being an elder seriously. That means teaching young people what they need to know and how they need to behave, even if they are not your own children.

Sometimes, when my show is done and I get off the air, there will be parents waiting in the lobby for me, usually with their teenage sons. They ask me to talk to their kids, and I am happy to do it.

One day, a woman who was confined to a wheelchair came to see me. Her teenage son was standing beside her, wearing his brand-new

Michael Jordan sneakers and looking irritated. His mother told me that he was mistreating her, refusing to listen to what she told him to do, and worrying her nearly to death.

I looked at him, then moved in close, until I was just a few inches away from his face. "Let me ask you a question," I said. "What are you going to do when the mortician comes in there and rolls that casket holding your mama out of that church? What are you going to do when the choir finishes singing, and they grab those flowers, swing that casket around, and roll your mama down the aisle, headed to the cemetery? Boy, that will be it!"

I told him he had a lot of nerve, disrespecting his mother. I said, "Look at your mama's feet, at her shoes, and now look at yours. How'd you get those Jordans? I'll tell you how. She worked hard to get them for you, treating you better than she treats herself."

Suddenly, that scowl on his face disappeared, and big tears started rolling down his face. His mother said she hadn't seen him cry in years. By the end of their visit, that kid was on his knees, crying and begging his mother for forgiveness, telling her how sorry he was and how he would try to do better.

We kept in touch and that boy turned his life around! His grades improved, and his mother says they have a much stronger, more positive relationship.

I don't want to make it seem like I'm just being hard on other people's kids. My own children can also be disrespectful, griping, and grumbling when I ask them to do chores. Sometimes they ignore what I say altogether. My children have had a lot of advantages, growing up in a large house with a swimming pool in the backyard and attending top-rated schools on landscaped campuses in the suburbs of Birmingham. But I think that for my kids, as well as a lot of other young people, the more money their parents make, and the more material possessions they receive, the more unappreciative and disrespectful they become.

That's unacceptable. I don't tolerate bad manners. Whatever your age, treating another person with respect is a matter of common decency. It's how we reinforce each other's inherent dignity. Each and every one of us is deserving of acknowledgment and courtesy.

When I finish a comedy show and walk out of the stage door, I'm as likely to encounter a crowd of men and women who are sleeping on the street as I am the suited-up, perfumed patrons that I've just entertained. Do you know why I have a lot of fans who happen to be homeless? It's because I always try to speak to everyone like they are a child of God.

I don't just give out cash and coats through the Rickey Smiley Foundation. I give advice, along with a few dollars, to the panhandlers on street corners. I visit shelters and offer encouragement to the residents, who may be struggling to stay hopeful. And when people who can't afford to buy tickets come and stand outside my shows, I invite them to my dressing room and tell them to enjoy the fruit and cookies and tea that the venue provides. I treat everyone with respect, because that is what each of us deserves.

As bad as it is to ignore or dismiss a stranger who just needs a helping hand, it is even worse to disrespect the people who make a difference in your life every day. And I'm not just talking to young people about their parents. There are other adults whom you might disregard. When was the last time you called your grandparents to check on how they were feeling? Did you tell the Uber driver you summoned with your mother's credit card thanks for the ride?

And how often do you offer words of appreciation to one of your teachers? So many young people refuse to give their teachers the respect they earn each and every time that they walk into a classroom.

You may not think it's necessary to acknowledge them, but years from now, when you impress a prospective employer with a historical fact that you were able to suddenly remember or feel at ease in a foreign country because you are able to speak the local language, you might think about the instructors who taught you those subjects. And it will most likely be too late to thank them.

I was young once, so I know that showing gratitude to the person teaching you art or algebra isn't exactly a priority. You're worrying about baseball practice, the grades that are going to show up on your report card, or how to impress that really cute new boy or girl. And while I knew that if I even rolled my eyes at an adult, I would get my behind beaten by my mother, I had plenty of classmates who thought it was cool to give their teachers a hard time.

But as rowdy as it sometimes got in the classroom when I was growing up in the 1970s and 1980s, the behavior was nothing like what some teachers have to endure nowadays. I've heard from my kids about young boys walking into class with their pants sagging, bothering the other students, and intimidating the instructors. *That* is just plain wrong.

Teachers sometimes stay up all night grading homework, and then they spend the next day trying to teach their students the ideas and problem-solving skills that they will need to compete in the world. And despite all of that hard work, many educators take home less in their paychecks than some parents spend on their kids' gadgets and toys.

I'm not kidding. My oldest daughter, D'essence, went to Spain Park High School in Hoover, Alabama. You would go to the student parking lot and see Range Rovers and souped-up trucks, while the teachers were driving Toyota Camrys. The one exception might have been the car that belonged to D'essence. It wasn't a wreck, but it definitely wasn't new. D'essence and the rest of my kids usually drive Toyota Corollas that are as old as they are. My rule is, if you want a new car, you either get a college degree and I'll buy you one, or you work for it and buy it yourself. My kids don't get up before dawn to support the household like I do, so they are not *entitled* to anything.

It hurts my heart to see the elders in our society treated disrespectfully. When I talk about elders, I'm not just referring to those who are gray haired and up in years. I'm referring to all those pillars of the neighborhood who have an impact on the up-and-coming generation. The village that helped raise me in Birmingham did not just consist of my relatives. It included the owner of the corner store, who sold us cinnamon buns and Popsicles in the summertime. It included the pastor at New St. James Baptist Church, the sanctuary that gave many members of my family their spiritual home and foundation. And the village included the many teachers who helped me to expand my knowledge, from the time I was a toddler until I attended Alabama State University in the late 1980s.

Many years ago, I thought I would actually become a teacher. I was an education major in college, and while it hadn't been my lifelong dream to stand in front of a blackboard, I'd always liked working around kids. I felt teaching would be a good, solid profession. But while I was still attending university, my comedy career took off and launched me in a different direction. I realize now that was a good thing, because if I walked into a classroom and had to face the type of bad behavior confronting so many teachers today, they'd have to haul me away so I wouldn't beat those bad kids.

I don't put up with disrespect. I check kids that are six or seven years old when they run up to me, pushing their fingers in my face, yelling, "Hey, you're Rickey Smiley!" I let them know that first of all, I don't want their fingers in my face, and secondly, I tell them, "It's *Mr.* Smiley to you. I don't know you, and you don't know me."

Then I mix love with the lesson. I give each of those kids a hug, and I also shake the boys' hands. I ask each of them what they want to be when they grow up. Then I let them know that I'm just trying to teach them what they need to know to accomplish their dreams, that they need to approach people with respect. "Let's try it one more time," I say gently. "Take a couple of steps back, and then say, 'Hello, are you Mr. Smiley?'"

Sometimes, the kids' parents get angry, but I feel that they should actually back me up and reinforce my message about good manners. When you meet a new person, especially in the South, it's "Mr.," "Mrs.," or "Ms." until they tell you differently. I'm a grown man, and I still operate that way, so there's no excuse for young people not to do the same. And in the end, it's not about being from a certain region of the country, or even about being polite. It's about creating a society in which everyone respects one another, no matter who you are.

I know a lot of you have young parents who are in their thirties or forties, and you can't imagine their not being around. But it's not guaranteed that your parents are going to always be here. As a matter of fact, the sure thing is that one day they won't be. When that time comes, I don't want you to have any regrets. I don't want you to wish that you'd shown them more respect. I don't want you to wish that you'd done more to acknowledge the support they gave and the sacrifices they made going to work every day to give you everything.

"Honor thy mother and thy father, that thy days may be long upon the land." That's in the Bible.

While you're young, you have plenty of time to change your behavior, to refocus your path, and to do what is right. I'm asking you teenagers who sit at the kitchen table talking into your phones instead of to the person sitting right beside you to put down your devices and pay attention to your parents. You might learn something. I'm telling you young people who spend half of your days immersed in video games to set aside the consoles and hug your mom and dad. You might be surprised by how good that makes you feel.

Try to make the best grades you can. Clean up your room without having to be told to do it a dozen times. Volunteer to help your parents make dinner, or, better yet, prepare the whole meal and give them a treat when they get home from work. And if you can't do anything else, show your parents, and all your elders, the respect that they deserve.

Honor thy mother and thy father, that thy days may be long upon the land. They'll appreciate you for it, and trust me, you'll be glad that you took the time to show how much you appreciate them.

IF YOU SPARE THE ROD,
TAKE OFF THE DOORS

I believe in tough love. I'm talking about a butt-spanking, allowance-taking, "You can't go anywhere but school, because you're grounded!" kind of love.

Every chore your son or daughter gets done doesn't call for a pat on the back. And your children should know there's a price to pay for sneaking out of the house, coming home after curfew, or playing football in the family room and breaking that vase your aunt Sandra left you in her will. Life isn't easy, and if you're soft on your children, the world and all its adversity will hit them hard. That pain is likely to be a thousand times worse than any scolding or spanking that they got at home.

Tough love doesn't mean beating your children within an inch of their lives, or never telling them how much you care about them. And it definitely doesn't mean acting as though your sons and daughters don't have voices that are worth listening to and respecting. I tell my sons, Brandon and Malik, and my daughters, D'essence and Aaryn, and my nephews, T. J., Terrell, and Craig, that I love them all of the time.

I ask them how they feel about what's going on in our society polit-

ically, what pressures they are dealing with in school, and any other issues that might be on their minds. It's important that young people
think critically, that they evaluate the world around them, and that they
know their observations have value. And your children should never
fear you to the point that they don't let you know when they are being
bullied at school, or that they are wondering how to behave when they
are out on a date.

But they should respect you. And they have to understand that
there are expectations that they need to meet and boundaries of behavior that they cannot cross. If they don't learn that from you, who
else is going to teach them?

That was the message I was trying to send to my nephew Craig
when I made him sleep in the garage. Yes, I said sleep in the garage.

Craig and I came into each other's lives when he was just five
years old. His mother, Candace, was an awesome stylist who worked
with me and other entertainers picking out what we should wear onstage, or to award shows and other red-carpet events. She could put
together scarves and caps, colors and fabrics that I never would have
thought of. She was talented and beautiful, and I think that we developed a bit of a crush on each other. But we sidestepped the romance
and kept our relationship grounded in business and friendship instead.

Candace was a single mother, and when she worked with clients
out of town, she usually had to bring her children with her. So one
weekend back in 2004 when I had a show coming up, Candace flew to
Birmingham to help me get my outfits together for the performance.
She brought Craig, and his older sister, Jurnee, with her.

I was raising my youngest child, Malik; my oldest son, Brandon;
and my daughter D'essence, so Craig and Jurnee blended right in. My
kids had a trampoline to jump on, a basketball hoop to dunk in, closets

stuffed with clothes, and a kitchen overflowing with all the Little Debbie Zebra Cakes they could ever want to eat.

But if those kids left their beds unmade, ignored the dishes piled in the sink, or didn't ask how high when I told them to jump, they got an earful from me—or worse. Candace saw the structure that I had in place, and she liked it.

Craig's and Jurnee's father was incarcerated, so they barely saw him. Candace wanted Craig in particular to have a strong male role model, a man who could show him how to conduct himself, as well as set him straight if he was misbehaving. I told her I would be happy to be a father figure to him and Jurnee. So, right after that first trip, Craig and Jurnee started visiting me regularly.

Weekends flowed into weekdays. Weeks turned into months, and eventually, in order for me to take a more formal role in guiding Craig's education and after-school activities, Candace and I decided it would be good for us to officially share legal custody. By the time Craig was in high school, he was living with me full-time in Birmingham.

When it came to bad kids, Craig was pretty low on the totem pole. When he was young, he might stay up late talking to Malik after I'd told them lights out, or slack off from time to time with his homework, but overall he was good-natured and did what he was supposed to do.

That is, until he turned sixteen. There's something about the teenage years that makes even the sweetest kids act like they've lost their minds. Suddenly, when it came to messing up, on a scale of one to ten, Craig shot straight to the top.

About a year before I sat down to write this book, Craig threw a party without my permission. To this day, I cannot figure out why he did that, because he should have known what was coming. Brandon had thrown his own party about ten years earlier, when he was in the eleventh grade, and he'd gotten the first one-way ticket to the concrete

I wasn't angry just because Brandon had thrown a party without my permission. What upset me most was that his lack of responsibility and his desire to be cool and show off in front of his classmates had put our whole family in jeopardy. What if somebody had drowned in the swimming pool? What if somebody had brought liquor into the house, drunk too much, and then had a car accident on the way home?

What Brandon, and later Craig, didn't get is that the seemingly simple act of inviting their buddies over to hang out at the house without parental supervision caused all kinds of security risks. Did they have their guests sign releases to relieve me of liability? Of course not. If Brandon and Craig had been doing what they were supposed to do, taking care of their chores and keeping up their grades, I would have let each of them have a party. I would have bought the soda, cooked the food, and hired the disc jockey. A party is something you earn. But they were hardheaded and rebellious, so they threw parties behind my back that they didn't deserve. That called for repercussions.

A police officer who pulls your son over for speeding won't let him slide like you do. The principal who calls your daughter into the office for cutting class won't just give her a gentle warning not to do it again. If your children drink beers when they're underage, tussle with a thug when they're better off walking away, or become sexually active before they're emotionally ready, the trajectory of their lives could change instantly. There are no do-overs.

My mother, my grandparents, and all of my uncles loved the heck out of me. But they also made sure that I knew that there would be people who didn't like me no matter how nice I was, and folks who'd try to make me question my abilities and dent my self-esteem. They let me know that I couldn't just sit around and cry about it, and I definitely couldn't buy into it. If people threw boulders in my path, I had to keep climbing, even if I skinned my knee, and even if I tripped on the way up.

Their tough love gave me thick skin. It made me strong enough to stick to my principles and not to badmouth other radio show hosts, even when they go on the air and talk about me. My no-nonsense upbringing gave me the fortitude to fight for years in Alabama's highest courts when an ungrateful woman tried to go after me for hundreds of thousands of dollars of back child support after I'd helped to raise her daughter.

My grandfather's love and lessons are what helped push me along the walkway and onto the plane when I left Birmingham for Dallas, unsure of what was waiting for me there. Tough love means you're preparing your children for the cutthroat world right outside the door, but also letting them know that they've always got a warm, welcoming place to come back home to.

So tough love meant Brandon was the first to get banished to the garage. I didn't think about buying him a cot. He slept on a mattress, and I made him stay out there for a couple of weeks.

Fast-forward ten years and now it was Craig's turn. Craig had actually been building up the reasons why he needed to be put out of the house. He'd gone into D'essence's room more than once and taken her cell phone when he had misplaced his. Now, I consider that straight-up stealing, so I was already figuring out how I was going to discipline him. Then he threw the party, and I knew that it was his turn to take up residence next to my Jeep.

I upgraded the accommodations a bit. I went to Walmart and bought one of those cots campers set up when they are off in the mountains on a hiking trip. Then I picked up enough food to last Craig a whole week. There was a different canned good and fruit for each day: chili and bananas, mixed vegetables and oranges, corned beef and peaches. If Craig ate all the food in one sitting, that was his choice. My thinking was that if you're acting like you're headed to prison, you might as well prepare for it by getting used to a bare-bones menu.

I gave Craig a small bowl, a fork, a knife, and a spoon. Then I set up a microwave on a shelf so that he could warm up the Campbell's Chunky soup that I threw in as a treat. He had three outfits that he could mix and match to wear to school, and he could come in the house three times a week to take a short shower. He had a small heater and a whole bunch of blankets.

That portable heater and those blankets didn't do him much good though on the days when I had to head to the radio station early in the morning. I'd go into the garage, push the button to automatically lift the door. I would take my time letting all the warmth in the garage slip away while the frosty morning air rushed in. Craig would be thrashing around, tugging those blankets over his head, trying as hard as he could to stay warm.

I didn't care. If you're stealing phones and endangering yourself, your friends, and your family by throwing parties you don't have permission to give, you deserve to be a little uncomfortable.

Craig stayed out there for three weeks. I replenished his pantry every Friday, and except for those showers, he didn't set foot in the house. When I wasn't home, Miss Pat, a woman I met at my church who now works for me and helps watch the kids, made sure of that.

The garage will set you straight. When I think about it, it's the perfect middle ground literally and metaphorically. It's the space between working your way back into the house and getting the hell out.

———

I KNOW IT might seem harsh making Craig and Brandon sleep on a cot or mattress in the garage instead of in their own beds. But I wasn't starving them or making them pitch a tent in a park. And I wasn't punishing them just to be mean. They had done something seriously wrong, and they deserved to suffer serious consequences.

Making them survive on canned food and sleep darn near outside for a few weeks was tough. But caring for them all the rest of the year, going to their ball games, cooking them a Southern feast every night, and disciplining them so that they didn't derail their dreams before their lives began—well, that's love.

You've got too many mothers and fathers who coddle their children, giving them everything they want, even when they don't deserve it. They're willing to risk their ability to pay the rent just so they can get Junior the latest Xbox. Mom and Dad might be feeling the concrete through the soles of their shoes, but their little princess prances around in a $200 pair of Uggs. These parents might have good intentions. Maybe when they were young, they were the kids at school wearing the discount jeans, the no-name sneakers, and the dollar-store caps. Maybe they got teased and don't want their kids to suffer the same experiences.

But you're not doing your children any favors by giving them everything they want and never punishing them when they misbehave. We've got to give our kids more of the discipline and guidance that we had as children, as opposed to giving them all the frivolous things that we think we missed out on.

———————

I COME FROM a family of military men. Sometimes the military chose them, drafting them to fight in a war overseas, but most of the time, the men in my family chose the military. They wanted good-paying jobs. They welcomed the GI Bill's financial help in paying for a college education. And during the days of Jim Crow, they wanted to escape the racism of Alabama.

The military has been a stepladder to the middle class for a lot of Americans. And for black people in particular, it has been a route to financial stability and respect that could be hard to find elsewhere, especially during the years of segregation.

When it comes to the history of black Americans' military service, my home state holds a special place. The Tuskegee Airmen, the legendary black air squadron that flew during World War II, were trained at Tuskegee Institute in Macon County, Alabama. Its pilots, bombardiers, and mechanics proved to the country how courageous and technically brilliant African-American men could be, and they made it harder going forward for our civil rights to be denied.

We've fought in every war, from the American Revolution to Afghanistan. Unfortunately, for too many years, black soldiers had to endure unequal treatment within the armed forces, and then disrespect or even violence when they came back home. But by the time my uncles enlisted, the military was one of the fairer playing fields in American life.

The military made you grow. You could go in surly and immature, and come out with a technical specialty and an understanding of how to strategize and survive under pressure. Those skills don't matter just on a military base or in a war zone. That type of focus, that ability to untangle problems, comes in handy every single day.

My grandfather Ernest was drafted toward the end of World War II. Twenty years later, my father, Ernest Jr., followed him into the army, while his brother Eugene, whom we kids called "Uncle Bro," joined the marines. My mother's brothers also became soldiers. My uncles Herbert and Blue fought in Vietnam, while my uncles Melvin and Dwight joined the military to jump-start their ability to make a living.

I think the military reinforced the kind of structure that my relatives had grown up receiving at home, at church, and around the neighborhood. The men in my family had rules about how to dress and how to behave.

You had to be sharp, with your shoes buffed, your shirt pressed, and your hair brushed. And my grandfather had better not have to tell you twice to empty that garbage can that was so full the trash was about to spill onto the kitchen floor.

I had to gather the plastic bags of trash in the kitchen, bedrooms, and bathrooms every night, pouring all of it into the metal can leaning against a wall outside the house. Then on garbage day, I'd drag the can out to the curb, where the sanitation workers picked it up. When I got home from school, I didn't dare walk through the front door until I'd dragged that garbage can back from the sidewalk and returned it to the side of the driveway where it belonged.

With my grandfather and uncles, there was no whining or crying allowed. Their motto was, "Get up, shake it off, and keep it moving." If Tony down the street knocked me down and snatched my M&M's, I couldn't go home until I'd gotten in his face and either taken that candy back or made Tony fork over enough change so that I could go to the store and buy a new bag.

My father's youngest brother, Anthony, was only six years older than me, so he was more like a big brother than an uncle. The family called him by his middle name, Bruce, and we shared a room when I stayed over at my grandparents' house. I really admired him. He was a fantastic athlete, and he went on to play football at the University of Alabama for the legendary coach Paul Bear Bryant. I have a photograph in my living room showing me sitting on Coach Bryant's lap and my uncle Bruce right beside us, smiling after accepting a four-year scholarship to attend the school.

Many days after school, some of the neighborhood kids and I would play pickup football in the front yard, and Bruce would watch us, yelling out tips (and disses) from the front porch. Sometimes, when I would get the wind knocked out of me and I looked toward him, tears in my eyes, he'd give me a hard stare.

"What are you doing?" he'd yell. "Get yo butt up and hit them back!" You'd better believe that I did what I was told.

The men in my family loved me and encouraged me, but they didn't baby me. They helped to make me the man that I am. I've never felt entitled. I've always expected that I would have to work hard and that my effort would ultimately be rewarded.

Being raised with such a strong work ethic has made me truly hate it when people feel that somebody owes them something undeserved, whether it's a pass for bad behavior, a professional break that they didn't earn, or an apology for some imaginary slight. Entitlement is a personality flaw that I see in so many people, and it's a characteristic that I resent more than any other. The only thing that someone owes you is basic courtesy, and if you don't know how to act, you don't deserve even that.

It wasn't just my relatives who gave my life rules and structure. When I was growing up in the 1970s, any adult in my world could whip my behind. If Miss Wells, one of the elders at New Mt. Olive Church, told me to get down from a tree that I had no business climbing and I didn't do it, she would grab me and a belt at the same time and then tear my butt up. Then, while I sat there crying, she'd strut over to my mother's house and tell her what I'd done, and I'd get another spanking when I got home. That was old-school.

But every once in a while, my grandmother Mattie wasn't in the mood for any- and everybody to discipline her baby. That's when the Smiley men, and their belief in tough love, intervened.

One afternoon, my peewee football team, the Tarrant Wildcats, was on the field. I got tackled and fell to the ground. That must have been about the third time in one practice that I'd gotten pinned down, and I was a little tired of getting hit. So I stayed on the ground, looking up to heaven and counting the seconds until the game was over. Then, *whomp!*

Coach Henderson took his foot and kicked me right in my behind. "Get your a-- up!" he screamed, the veins popping in his forehead.

I found out later that when my grandmother Mattie saw that, she was practically knocking folks over as she climbed down from the bleachers, so she could stomp onto the field and give Coach Henderson a kick in *his* backside. But my grandfather Ernest stopped her.

"Leave him alone," he said, grabbing her arm. "Coach is going to help make a man out of him."

Now, that day at Tarrant Park, lying on the field and gasping for breath, I was siding with my grandmother's point of view. But over time, as I became more resilient, not just on the football field but also in other parts of my life, I came to appreciate my grandfather's view. Years later, I found myself relaying my grandfather's message when my own child Malik was out on the football field.

I noticed that Malik would miss passes, flub throws, and just wimp out whenever the playing got too rough. After seeing that same pattern over the course of a couple of practices, I knew that I had to have a talk with his coach.

I felt I understood what was going on. By then, I was a well-known radio personality. I also sponsored the team: I wrote the checks that bought the uniforms and filled the coolers with Gatorade and Popsicles, and had already committed to paying for the food and trophies that would be handed out at the end-of-the-season team banquet. So it wasn't that hard to figure out that Coach might have been a little nervous about getting in my son's face. I had to let him know that letting Malik slide wasn't acceptable.

When practice ended and the kids were heading to their parents' cars or to the clubhouse to change, I pulled Coach aside.

"We've got to talk," I said to him quietly. "I know that Malik is Rickey Smiley's son, but I need you to grab him by the face mask and put your foot in his a--! If I wanted him to be soft, I would've signed him up for needlepoint at the YWCA."

Coach just looked at me and didn't say a word. But at the next practice, Malik didn't know what hit him. If he stayed down on the ground too long, he got yelled at until he got up. When he kept dropping the ball, he had to stay after practice to do extra drills. If he talked back, he had to drop to the ground and do push-ups. Everything had changed. He was getting a big dose of discipline, a big helping of tough love.

Just as the whole community has a role in raising all of our children, offering them encouragement, and helping out any child who is hungry or hurting, I also believe that the village—of teachers, coaches, mentors, and ministers—should be allowed to hand out discipline. Kids need to know that the same rules they are required to respect at home apply when they're walking around the neighborhood, hanging out at the shopping mall, or going to school. And if they break them, other adults have the authority to put them in check.

In my opinion, that even applies to spanking. Yes, I believe in corporal punishment. I know it's not politically correct to do or say, but I've whipped the behinds of every one of my kids. The only one I didn't have to spank was D'essence.

She threw one tantrum when she was about two years old. I carried her into her room, held down her legs until she stopped bucking and thrashing, and then I went and grabbed my belt.

"The next time you act up like that, I'm going to use this to tear your little behind up," I said.

Do you know that little girl said, "Yes, sir," like she was a marine and I was a drill sergeant? From that day on, I never had to show her my belt again. I think she figured out early that I was crazy. She steered so clear of me that she wouldn't even attempt to push my buttons. When I would tell Malik or Brandon or Craig to go to bed, they would take their time getting there, or once they were under the covers, they'd look back at me when I went to check on them like they were trying to challenge me by keeping their eyes open.

But D'essence? She'd get in the bed and act like she was knocked out five seconds later. Her eyes would be squeezed so tight there were creases in her forehead. I knew that she hadn't fallen asleep that fast and that nobody sleeps that hard, but D'essence wasn't playing. She didn't want any trouble from me.

Malik and Aaryn were a different story. Aaryn could be a certifiable brat, demanding Rice Krispies at three o'clock in the morning and screaming bloody murder when I told her no. "I want my mommy," she'd say, crying big crocodile tears. "Hold on," I'd say, jumping out of bed and heading to my closet.

I'd pull out my trusty belt. "Here's your mommy right here."

Sometimes she'd get a spanking. Other times, she'd get the message, stop making noise, and slink back to her room.

But Malik, well, he was just bad. My belt was so familiar with his backside that it practically took on his shape. His only fear, when he was four or five years old, was bubbles—the kind that are passed around as a favor at birthday parties. If you blew some toward him, Malik would be terrified and take off running. But he'd go out in the backyard and pick up anything creeping, crawling, or slithering. I'm talking about a raccoon, a skunk, even a snake.

One time, he grabbed a snake near the head, let it wrap around his arm like a wristwatch, and strolled back into the living room. "Dad!" he screamed. "Look what I got!"

I stopped dead in my tracks. Then I spoke softly, shooing him and his new pet back out the door and telling him to let the snake go. As soon as that snake had slithered back into the bushes where it belonged and Malik came back into the house, I had my belt waiting for him. He had to learn that our living room wasn't an annex of the Birmingham Zoo.

I got plenty of spankings when I was a kid, and not just from my family. I got paddled by my coaches; my sixth-grade teacher, Miss Avery; and my elementary school principal, Rosa P. Hanks. A sore backside didn't permanently stop me from acting up, but it definitely made me push pause on immediately doing something else that would get me in more trouble.

There are a couple of things that our schools should bring back. One is prayer. It's good for children to have a spiritual foundation that extends beyond the church, the mosque, or wherever their families might worship. And the other thing missing in our educational system is the permission for a teacher or principal to give a misbehaving student a good smack on the behind.

Kids nowadays don't expect to face consequences for their actions. I'll never forget the words I heard from a speaker at a Tavis Smiley event that I attended years ago. The woman on the stage said teachers are afraid of principals, principals are afraid of superintendents, the superintendents are afraid of the parents, and the kids? Well, they're not afraid of anybody.

It's true. A lot of children will do what they want, and if you even look like you're raising your hand in their direction, they're whipping out their smartphone and threatening to call Child Protective Services.

Forget spanking. You can't even scold a child who's acting up. That's why I seldom invite guests to my home who have kids. If you tell

Bae Bae's daughter to stop jumping on your dining room table, Bae Bae will come after you. "You hurt Little Bae Bae's feelings! She's a good kid!"

Her feelings? What about my dining room table? If Little Bae Bae doesn't know better than to jump on someone's furniture, and you don't have enough backbone to tell her to get down, then I'm stepping up and stepping in.

Sometimes Little Bae Bae will actually curse you out. So will her mother, Big Bae Bae. And Miss Bae Bae, her grandmother, will stop by the next night on her way to a bid whist party to read you the riot act about disciplining her little darling.

Too many parents are afraid to give their sons and daughters tough love, or to empower other responsible adults to do the same. But what sense does that make?

Kids are going to push boundaries and sometimes just simply misbehave. It's up to us, their elders who know better, to let them know when they've strayed too far and to then make them so uncomfortable that they don't do it again.

TWO YEARS AGO I gave my oldest son, Brandon, a car for Christmas.

We'd already done our usual holiday ritual of getting up early and taking gifts to the less fortunate all over Birmingham. Now we were back home, and the kids were gathered around the tree, tearing off wrapping paper, ripping off ribbons, and taking selfies with all of their presents.

Brandon looked through the pile of boxes and didn't find anything. "Where's my gift?" he asked, a worried look crossing his face. I reached into my pocket, pulled out a set of keys, and tossed them to him.

After we'd come home, I'd asked Big Ro', my childhood friend who was now my security guard, to drive Brandon's car to the house from where we'd parked it down the hill. Brandon ran outside and found a tan 1999 Tahoe sitting in the driveway. He was ecstatic.

Fast-forward a few months. My niece Porshé was earning top grades in school, working a part-time job, and always helping her mother around the house, without even being asked. She was just a sweet, energetic, hardworking kid. Brandon, meanwhile, was steadily messing up.

One day, I'd discovered a bong in his closet. That got him grounded for a week. Then, days later, and for the second time, I found ashes and beer cans in the back of his SUV.

The morning I made that discovery, my cell phone rang. It was my sister calling to chat. We caught up, talking about work and how some of our relatives were doing. Then she mentioned how much running around Porshé had to do, hopping the bus or asking for rides to get between work, school, and home.

The next day, I called Porshé.

"Hey," I said, "ask your mother to bring you by the house."

Then I yelled out to Brandon, who was upstairs in his room. I told him to take the Tahoe and get it detailed, and I meant the works, from Armor All on the tires to Carpet Fresh on the car mats.

"That's a good idea, Dad," Brandon said, grabbing some cash from me and rushing happily out the door.

By the time Brandon got back a couple of hours later, Porshé and my sister were there, sitting with me in the living room.

"Hey, Brandon!" I said. "Hand me those keys." He tossed them to me. Then I tossed them to Porshé.

Brandon was in shock, and Porshé looked like she didn't know whether to jump for joy or break down crying.

"You need a car, don't you?" I asked her. "You don't want it?"

Porshé felt bad for her cousin, but she wasn't stupid. She walked out the door, jumped in the driver's seat, and never looked back, a little smile creeping around the edges of her mouth. Brandon was back to riding the bus.

Porshé was doing everything right and didn't have a car that she really needed, while Brandon had gotten this wonderful gift and abused it. So I took the SUV from somebody who didn't appreciate it, didn't keep it clean, and smoked and drank inside of it, and gave it to somebody who actually deserved it.

I GUESS YOU can tell by now that my creativity doesn't just stop with my comedy routines. But some of my methods of punishment are borrowed from the older people I grew up with. One is spanking. The other is taking the doors off of my kids' bedrooms.

Malik and Craig snuck out of the house one evening. Then another time, Craig snuck out and Malik lied to cover for him. It's too bad that they weren't as smart as they were bold. First, Miss Pat was staying at the house, and there is not a door that creaks or a car that starts that Miss Pat doesn't hear. Secondly, I have a security system and cameras posted all over my property. Anybody coming in the house or leaving is captured right there on *Candid Camera*.

So, since Malik and Craig couldn't be trusted and needed to be watched like a couple of babies, I got a screwdriver and took their bedroom doors off the frames. Then I got some beads, like hipsters used to hang back in the seventies, and draped them so that they had a veil of privacy. Their rooms were across the hall from each other, so if they got lonely and wanted someone to commiserate with, they could push back the beads and give each other a pout.

At least they weren't sleeping in the garage.

Several months later, Craig moved out to go live with his grand-mother, and Malik headed back to military school. Until then, those doors stayed off.

A lot of parents worry that they will lose their children's love if they are strict with them. But I know firsthand that the opposite is true. They may be mad at you for a while. Maybe, if you're separated from their other parent, they'll talk about how they'd prefer to go live with their mom or dad.

But when they calm down, once their backside or pride stops hurt-ing, you'll realize you've earned their respect. They'll appreciate that you loved them enough to be tough.

Malik, who'd misbehaved and slacked off a lot in public school, was enrolled in a military academy starting in the seventh grade, and he has excelled. He wound up following the military tradition of the men in our family sooner than any of us would have expected. Malik loves the structure so much that he actually sought out a transfer to an-other military school with an even stricter regimen. When he comes home on the weekends, he literally stands at attention in the dining room, with his hands clasped behind his back. And he's up at five a.m., his bed neatly made, because he's used to getting up before dawn and jumping into formation.

He's gotten so tough, I sometimes wonder if I need to take steps to soften him up.

One evening, we were watching *Titanic*. There's that final scene when the character Rose, who'd survived the ship's sinking, goes to sleep in her bed as an old woman. Then the *Titanic* comes back to life, and she walks up the stairs and finds her lost love, Jack, waiting for her by the clock. Man, every single time I watch that, I scream, "Sweet

Jesus, come take me right now!" and bawl like a baby. The only other time a movie makes me cry that much is when I'm watching *The Color Purple* and the character Shug Avery walks into her father's church, singing for his forgiveness.

But that night, while I was sitting there blowing my nose and wiping my eyes, do you know what Malik was doing? He stared at the screen, looking bored half to death, then went back to scrolling through Instagram. I mean, if you watch *Titanic* and you don't cry, you need counseling.

Titanic aside, I respect the strong, disciplined young man that Malik's become. I see the hard work my elders put into raising me, as well as the hard work I put into raising all of my children, reflected in him.

Sometimes, I even hear my own words coming out of my children's mouths. "That dog behind the fence barks at the mailman, but the mailman doesn't bark back," D'essence will say. "If he did, he couldn't get on with doing his job. And when he's back home with his family, that dog is still stuck behind that fence."

That's one of my favorite lessons. Don't worry about what folks might be saying about you. Take care of what you're supposed to do, and you'll be the winner in the end.

I've also seen D'essence announce to her college roommates that it's cleanup day, and she'll make sure all those other young women pick their jeans up off the floor, pull out the vacuum cleaner, and clean the bathroom before they head out to Starbucks or Jamba Juice. That makes me happy.

Every Sunday, I cook a big dinner. My grandfather Ernest usually sits at the head of the table, and the rest of the chairs are filled with my kids, some of our other relatives, and maybe a couple of family friends. When we're done plowing through chicken and dumplings, macaroni

and cheese, and whatever else I've prepared that day, without my saying a word, my children clear the table, wash the dishes, and scrub the
kitchen until there's not a wayward crumb.

"Boy," my guests will say with admiration. "Rickey's got those children trained!"

"Yes," I say with a nod and a smile, "I do."

THE MYTH OF THE
DEADBEAT DAD

O n my radio show, Father's Day is a cause for a major celebration.

It always falls on a Sunday in June, and we air during the
week, but I make sure that first thing Monday morning, and often for
days after, I recognize and honor all of the wonderful fathers in our
communities and around the country.

I give a shout-out to the men who are picking their children up
from school and coaching their sons' Little League baseball teams. I
give props to the guys who are braiding their daughters' hair in the
morning and then teaching them how to ride a bike in the afternoon. I
acknowledge the dudes who work hard at one job during the day and
then turn around and drive Lyft or Uber at night, all so that their children want for nothing.

There are so many loving, giving fathers who are unsung. I want
each and every one to know that I see them.

Usually, in honor of Father's Day, I have different dads come on
my radio show to talk about all that they do. I ask them to speak directly to the men out there who aren't stepping up to the plate, em-

phasizing how they give the rest of us a bad name and that they need to handle their responsibilities.

I invite attorneys to come on my show, as well, because some men need to be reminded that they have a legal—as well as God-given—right to see their children, regardless of whether they are romantically involved with the kids' mother. Children don't belong more to their mothers than they do their fathers, and young people need both parents in their lives to grow into the healthy, whole adults that we want each of our sons and daughters to become.

Too often, fathers get a bad rap. We have a culture that still paints us as part-time parents, working all day and barely acknowledging our children at night. There's still an assumption that if parents split up, the men can get a few hours with their sons and daughters every other weekend, and that is more than enough—or all that we deserve. In no way is that right.

There are countless fathers out there working a nine-to-five who can't wait to get home in the evening to spend quality time with their kids. They capture every violin recital with their smartphones, hog the front row at every performance by their kid's band, and scream loud enough to make the ceiling shake at every football, baseball, and basketball game.

And if they break up with their wives or girlfriends and are denied the opportunity to see their sons and daughters, those same dads will fight like hell for those children. I know, because I damn sure fought like hell to see mine.

I WAS GETTING ready to head back to classes at Alabama State when my girlfriend Nicole told me that she was pregnant.

It was May 1989, and the two of us had been dating for about three years. Nicole was beautiful, with honey-dipped skin and high, delicate cheekbones. We'd met when I was a senior in high school and she was a freshman. We thought that we were in love, because we were too young and the feelings were too new for us to really know any better.

When times were good, they were great. But we argued a lot, too, over silly stuff, like my standing too close to her friend Jocelyn when we went to McDonald's, or her grinning a little too long when Ajaye gave her a hug after he scored the winning touchdown in the game be-tween Ramsay and Woodlawn High. We'd break up, then make up, practically every other week.

Then, somewhere along the way, Nicole began to date another guy named Michael. We would get back together, but it seemed like Mi-chael was always there, waiting in the wings.

When Nicole told me that she was pregnant, it knocked the breath out of me. I was still in school. I had little side jobs that I worked to help pay my tuition and to buy my clothes and meals, but I definitely wasn't rolling in money. Still, I never considered walking away. I'd lost my biological dad when I was a little boy, but I'd had a grandfather and a whole bunch of uncles who'd stepped into the breach. I had to figure things out and prepare to be a dad.

Nicole eventually transferred from Ramsay to Ensley High School, which had a maternity program. And I was dutiful. I would go with her to every doctor's appointment at the Eastern Health Center where she'd get her blood pressure checked and the nurse or attending physi-cian would make sure all was good with the baby. On the way back home, I'd mull over in my mind what jobs I could stitch together so that I would have enough money to do what needed to be done when the baby came.

But when Nicole finally went into labor, on February 7, 1990, nobody even bothered to tell me. It was her cousin who finally called and said that Nicole had given birth to a baby boy. She'd named him Brandon.

I immediately called Nicole's hospital room. How was she doing? How was Brandon? Why hadn't someone called, so I could have been with her at the hospital?

This should have been one of the most beautiful days of my life, but her response made it one of the darkest. Nicole said that she was sorry, but she didn't believe that the baby was mine.

It was like I'd prepared day and night for a big job interview, studying the company, practicing my presentation in front of a mirror, reading up on the competition, only to find out at the last minute that the position had already been filled. My disappointment felt like that, only one hundred times worse.

All of that planning, all of that going to bed with butterflies in my stomach and waking up scared—but a little excited, too—was for nothing. I'd gone with Nicole to every doctor's appointment. I'd bought baby blankets and bottles. I'd told my family a baby was coming. What the hell did she mean that he wasn't mine?

She said that the baby's father was Michael. The guy waiting in the wings was now front and center.

I was devastated. It was the lowest point in my life. I would just sit on my grandmother Ada's porch wondering where my life was headed. My car had broken down. I was going to need to take a break from school. And my mother was in the grip of drug addiction, disappearing for days at a time.

I sank into a deep depression. There were moments when I wanted to die. Only church, the thought of hearing some words from the Good Book and singing some sweet praise, kept me going.

One Sunday, I went to church and took a seat in the balcony's front row. I peered over the railing and saw Nicole and her mother downstairs. In her mother's arms was a baby. It was Brandon.

I looked away briefly as the congregation stood up to sing, and I swear that when I looked back Brandon's large brown eyes locked on mine. Finally, his grandmother noticed, too. She followed his gaze right up to the balcony.

Brandon just kept on looking at me, and I kept on looking at him. Our eyes never wavered.

I'M NOT IN denial. There are definitely some bad fathers out there, men who create children but somehow don't think they have any responsibility once those children come into this world.

I remember taking Harlan, a little boy I mentored, to the barbershop and his father thanking me for getting him a haircut when he should have been the one spending time with his son. I remember my sister Karon's ex-husband watching me walk his daughter ReeRee down the aisle, because I had been her dad all the years he'd been gone, not doing a thing for his beautiful girls.

I'm not sure there's anyone lower than a father who won't take care of his children. I was thinking just the other day how a giraffe, living in the wild, living on instinct, has sense enough to care for its young. Yet there are human beings, with all the mental power and consciousness that we are supposed to possess, who abandon their children.

How do you have sense enough to figure out how to drive a car, or how to pass an exam, but then turn off your mind, your sense of right and wrong, when it comes to your own child? How do you not take care of someone who carries your name, who carries your genes, who carries a piece of your soul? It's unnatural. It's not human.

I shake my head when I think of the father who doesn't want to be involved with his children when they're young but pops up like a jack-in-the-box when his son becomes a football star or his daughter earns her PhD. Now, when the hard work has been done, he wants a taste of the glory.

I'm sorry. If you're not there to put Band-Aids on the bruises, to give counsel during a breakup, to teach the rules of the road and those of life, then you don't deserve to pose in the graduation pictures or stand up there grinning after the championship game.

Still, for every neglectful dad, there are five, ten, twenty more men who give parenting their all. And there are many men who will be there for a child whether or not he or she is theirs.

When the shock about Brandon not being mine started to wear off, I would still see Nicole socially from time to time. So I got to see Brandon, too. He'd be plopped on the floor at her family's apartment in the Avondale Housing Projects, or sitting in his high chair making a mess with his applesauce and carrots. I would tease his mom.

"Man, Nicole," I'd say, laughing. "Why is your baby so fat?"

It must have been divine intervention that I happened to be there when Brandon took his first steps. I'd stopped by the apartment, and Brandon was struggling, grabbing hold of a chair, then falling down, grabbing on to his mother's leg and then tumbling over. Then, finally, he grabbed hold of something, steadied himself, and put one leg in front of the other.

He was walking. I was there. I had seen it.

Life kept moving. Nicole and Michael were planning on getting married. My comedy career was taking off. Brandon was getting older. He called me Mr. Rickey.

Nicole and I remained friendly enough that she would let me take Brandon out sometimes. He and I would go get ice cream, or he would just ride around with me in my car, the breeze rushing through the windows and keeping us cool on a summer afternoon.

But after a while, something strange started happening. People would pull me to the side at the ice-cream parlor, at the store, or on the street. They knew the story. They knew the deal. But still, they asked the question.

"Are you sure he isn't your son?"

People said that Brandon had my nose, my eyes, my mannerisms, even my laugh. They saw my face in his.

I had largely made peace with my disappointment that I wasn't Brandon's father. But I had always had a nagging feeling deep in the pit of my soul that something wasn't right. I got suspicious.

One day, I was talking to one of my uncles.

"I saw that little boy," he said. "He looks just like you did when you were that age. I would have thought he was you, if I didn't know you were grown. I think that's your son."

By the time Brandon was six, my internal radar was beeping like crazy. He was no longer just a little kid who bore a strong resemblance to me. Now he looked like my mini twin.

I started questioning Nicole. How did she know he wasn't mine? She'd get angry, we'd argue, and then we wouldn't talk for a couple of months. After the second or third time that happened, I knew I had to find another way to get to the truth.

I went to speak to an attorney named Henry Penick. "I think I have a son," I told him, "but his mother is denying it. Are there any legal steps that I can take so I can be sure?"

He said I could get a court order for a paternity test. Within days, Nicole was served and ordered to submit a sample of Brandon's DNA. I was actually walking into the facility where his sample and mine were taken just as Brandon and Nicole were walking out. We waved at each other. Based on that interaction, you'd never know that it had taken a court order to make those tests happen.

A week or two later, Mr. Penick gave me a call. "Where are you?" he asked. "Can you come see me right away?" Before he'd even hung up the phone, I was speeding toward his office.

The results were in. And right there, in black and white, the paper said that it was 99.9 percent certain that I was Brandon's father.

I was so damn angry. If I hadn't taken some deep breaths to try to calm myself, I might have done something that landed me in jail. I left the lawyer's office and went straight to the hair salon where Nicole worked.

"You are a liar!" I yelled after she'd stepped out of the salon. "You lied to me for seven years!" I handed her the paperwork.

After seven years of denial, after forcing me to go to court to get proof that Brandon was my son, do you know what she had to say?

"I don't appreciate you coming to my job."

That was it. No apology. No explanation.

I just snatched the paper back and stormed off. I had more important things to do than fight with her. I needed to see my child.

I drove straight to the apartment that Nicole shared with her mother and Brandon. I ran to the door, rang the bell, and pushed the paper into her mother's hands. There was no preamble, no warm-up. "I am Brandon's father," I said, rushing inside.

While Nicole's mother stood there in shock, I looked over at Brandon, who was sitting right there in the living room. He'd heard what I'd said.

I walked over, knelt down, and put my hands on his face. "Could I have a hug?" I asked him. He reached out, and we held each other for a long time.

I stayed over for a while. Brandon and I played ball for a bit outside, and my anger at Nicole started to subside, dissolving into the happiness I felt now that I had proof that what I had long suspected was true. It was all out in the open. Now our father-and-son relationship could truly begin. I was no longer Mr. Rickey. From that day on, Brandon called me "Dah," for "Daddy."

It was time for Brandon to meet the rest of his family. My mother and my grandparents all knew that I was taking a paternity test. But when the results proved that I really was Brandon's dad, it was still kind of shocking to everyone. They suddenly had a new grandson and great-grandson, who was already seven years old.

When I introduced him to my grandparents Mattie and Ernest, it was a bit awkward at first. My grandfather shook Brandon's small hand like he was a little man. It was one of the few times that I'd ever seen him at a loss for words. We took some pictures, stayed a few minutes, then headed out to see my mother.

Her reaction was the opposite of my granddad's. My mother scooped Brandon up the second she saw him. I could barely pry him out of her arms when it was finally time to go. He didn't want to leave her, either, and even now that Brandon is grown, they are still incredibly close.

That was the first of so many beautiful days. Brandon got to know all his new aunts, cousins, and uncles, and he even met Mama Cherry, my grandfather's mother, not long before she died. I mean, how many children get to meet, touch, and kiss their great-great-grandparent?

In the months that followed, after I got off the air at 95.7, I would head over to Nicole's and pick Brandon up, and we'd drive around holding hands the whole ride. I taught him how to throw and catch a football. And he would go with me to some of the clubs where I performed, where he sat backstage and played with his toys. We loved each other from the start.

Nicole was still with Michael, but she acknowledged that things had changed forever. She told Brandon that now he had two dads. Since Michael had always been in Brandon's life, I didn't mind. I could live with that.

But so many good things don't come easily. After all the years it took for Brandon and me to know our true bond, it was going to take a few more for us to be together without interference. Nicole wasn't going to make it simple.

When I'd been "Mr. Rickey," a casual family friend who dropped by from time to time, seeing Brandon was no problem. Now that I had proof that Brandon was actually my child, spending time with him suddenly became an issue. Soon, Nicole stopped letting me take him places. Sometimes, she wouldn't even let me talk to him. I knew that I had no choice. I had to go to court.

———

THE SO-CALLED SYSTEM is hard on fathers. This is a legal system that for many years automatically gave custody to a mother, regardless of her behavior or circumstances. This is a system that will put a man in jail for not paying child support, never mind if the amount is more than he can reasonably pay. Or that, despite those checks, his ex-wife still won't let him talk to his daughter. I'm not saying that a man should get away with not financially supporting his kids, but I ask you, what man can come up with child support if he is locked behind bars?

It's a system that often leaves a father's fate up to the whims and biases of whoever is sitting on the bench. I once heard that there was a judge who said his reason for always awarding custody to the mother was that he'd never seen a calf follow a bull. Can you believe that? If you don't get somebody who has an open mind, who takes the idea of balancing the scales of justice seriously, you can be in real trouble.

My case for joint custody of Brandon wound up in front of a judge who I heard had a reputation for being unsympathetic to men in general. When I had a hearing, I would sit in the back of her courtroom waiting for my turn, and I would watch her order one father after the other to be sent to jail for being behind on his child support payments. Why couldn't a man who might have run into some financial problems be ordered to take a parenting class or given a new deadline to get paid up? To me, the punishment didn't fit the so-called crime.

Thankfully, laws are changing. There are fathers who are getting full custody of their children, or at least equal time to spend with them. But in the 1990s, it was still an uphill battle.

And there were some mothers who took full advantage of the biases in their favor. I met men whose ex-wives got away with not even allowing them to talk to their kids on the phone. I've heard stories of ex-girlfriends falsely claiming that their kids' fathers had abused their children—the most vicious accusation you can make.

I don't care what happened in the relationship. Lying in such a terrible way to deny a father the chance to help raise his children is shameful. And the stigma of the deadbeat dad too often gets attached to men who are doing everything in their power to be involved in their children's lives.

I asked the judge for a schedule that would give me as much time with Brandon as possible, to make up for the seven years that I had lost. Could I get an extra weekend here or there, or a day or two during the week? Her answer: I could see Brandon every other weekend, every other holiday, Father's Day, and one month in the summer. Any additional time with Brandon would be up to Nicole.

That limited schedule was supposed to be the deal from the time Brandon was seven until he was at least thirteen and could possibly say who he wanted to live with. What kind of sense did that schedule make? If you wanted to do the biological math, Brandon was 50 percent mine. So why couldn't he be with me at least half of the time?

If a child is just hanging out with a babysitter, why can't his father take him to get a haircut or a sandwich, even if it's not his designated day to visit? Why can't he be the one to watch his child, instead of some lady who's being paid five dollars an hour?

And when a child becomes a teenager and starts testing limits or getting a little out of control, there's only so much a part-time dad can or will do. I mean, think about it. How does a dad discipline a child that he barely gets to see? If you get just four days a month with your son or daughter, you want to shoot baskets and go to the movies. You don't want to punish your kids and have them sitting in their rooms all day, when you haven't seen them in two weeks.

A kid who barely sees their father may not listen to him, anyway. How much can you teach a child if you pick them up at five p.m. every other Friday and have to get them back to their mother on Sunday by three? What kind of influence are you going to have? An every-other-week visitation schedule doesn't work for anybody.

When my schedule kicked in, Brandon's mother stuck to it like it was the Constitution. She wouldn't give me any leeway, not for any reason.

One time, I stopped by to take Brandon around the corner to McDonald's. Nicole wasn't there, but her mother, the same woman who had watched Brandon stare at me from a church pew when he was a baby, and hugged me the day I brought the papers proving that I was his father, had evidently been given instructions.

No, she said. It wasn't my day to see him, and Nicole said that I couldn't take Brandon anywhere unless it was officially part of the visitation schedule. Then she shut the door in my face, right in front of Brandon, who was standing there behind her with tears in his eyes.

I couldn't take my eight-year-old son around the corner to get a Happy Meal? It was outrageous.

There were other times, when I was running late from an appearance, or had another business engagement, that I would send a good friend to pick up Brandon. Even though Nicole knew the guy and that he could be trusted, she wouldn't let him bring Brandon to me.

Yet if Nicole had something she wanted to do with Brandon on my designated weekend, it might mean that I got to see him on Saturday afternoon and then had to get him back home by the next evening. Often, at the end of those abbreviated visits, Brandon would cry. He felt cheated, and so did I.

It hurt to see him hurt. It hurt to be denied the right to see my child when I wanted to.

So I finally stopped asking. I started saying, "I'm not going to make special requests to see my son, because he's mine. I'm going to knock on the door, pick him up when I feel like it, and bring him back when I'm good and ready." Brandon and I were going to be together when we wanted to be, and I didn't care if it was Thursday afternoon, Tuesday night, or on back-to-back Saturdays.

First, I gave some straight talk to Nicole's grandmother, who often watched Brandon. I reminded her that I was Brandon's dad, not some stranger, and instead of playing security guard, she might want to tell her granddaughter that whatever her issues were with me, she wasn't going to keep me away from Brandon.

Nicole's grandmother got the message. She was willing to defy her granddaughter's wishes because she knew those demands were wrong. Nicole's grandmother and I actually still get along. I even send her $150 a month to help with bills.

But she's not the only one I had to set straight. I got bolder and bolder with everyone. One time, I was the grand marshal for the Magic

City Classic, the annual football face-off between Alabama State and Alabama A&M University. Thousands of people attend the parade before the game, and like just about everyone else in Birmingham, Brandon was going to be there.

I told him that when he saw me, he should call my name and come jump on the float. The day of the big game, just like clockwork, Brandon yelled, "Dah!" and then leaped onto the moving platform. I yelled out to his aunt who had brought him that I would get him home before dark. And that was it. He didn't ask for permission, and neither did I.

I started showing up wherever Brandon was going to be, whether it was Tae Kwon Do practice or a dodgeball game in the neighborhood.

Nicole didn't like it. She threatened to call the police. But I called her bluff. I dared her to do it. She couldn't style enough hair to earn all the money she would need to hire lawyers to keep me away from my son.

That battle over Brandon lasted about five years. Nicole, Michael, and Brandon eventually moved to Atlanta, and I petitioned the court for a new custody arrangement. Georgia allowed thirteen-year-olds to say where they wanted to live, and Brandon told the judge there that he wanted to live with me. Nicole would have to prove that I was unfit, which she couldn't do. And so I won full custody of my oldest son.

I'd fought Nicole until she couldn't fight anymore. She had to throw in the towel. I finally had the law on my side and won the right to parent my son without Nicole's being able to oversee and control the situation.

And Brandon was worth every ounce of my efforts. Whenever I saw him, it was sheer joy. I would always be playing Bill Withers's uplifting song "Lovely Day" when he jumped in my truck, because now that I was about to spend time with him, the day had become unbelievably beautiful. Then I'd play "You Make Loving Fun" by my favorite group, Fleetwood Mac. Twenty years later, that's still Brandon's favorite song.

The first time Brandon ever set foot on a plane, it was with me. I picked him up one day when he and his mother were still living in Birmingham. I was pretty sure that he hadn't flown before, but I asked him just to make sure.

"No, sir," he said.

I told him that we were going to go to the airport and watch the planes take off and land. But when we got there, we boarded a flight instead. We were headed out of town, to the amusement park Busch Gardens. I took pictures of him looking out of the window, seeing the view above the clouds for the first time. It felt like a magic carpet ride.

When we landed, we had the time of our lives. We rode those roller coasters at Busch Gardens until we couldn't ride them anymore. Then we went to the hotel, ordered a pepperoni pizza, and fell asleep. First thing the next morning, we jumped on a Southwest flight back to Birmingham.

———

THERE ARE MOTHERS out there who are amazing, not only because they are doing an awesome job parenting in their own right, but also because they have sense enough to know that kids—all kids—need a father.

There are women like Elizabeth, the mother of my children D'essence and Malik. Also Candace, whose son, Craig, and daughter, Jurnee, I raised as my own. There are women like Tamika, who is the mother of my youngest daughter, Aaryn. Also Angel and Telisha, the mothers of T. J. and Terrell, my best friend's sons. They were great role models and caregivers for their children, and even more incredible, they were willing to share their wonderful sons and daughters with me.

All of us have to look out for each of our children's best interests. It's only human to sometimes get caught up in petty squabbles, to want to get back at someone who you feel has done you wrong. But we can't allow children to be pawns in those fights. We can't make them suffer because of our selfishness.

I'm not superman. The treatment that I endured trying to gain more access to my son made me angry. And I believe that all that tussling back and forth took a toll on Brandon, who's struggled to find his way as an adult.

I've been angry about all the wasted time and all the wasted energy. Those are two things that you can never get back. What could Brandon and I have been doing on those afternoons that I spent in court? What could we have been cooking up to read or design when I was sitting there stewing about having to take him back to his mother the next day, after I hadn't seen him in two weeks?

But I had to move forward, and I had to forgive. Otherwise, even more time and energy would have continued to slip away.

Nicole and Michael had a daughter, Taylor, a decade after Nicole had Brandon. She is an amazing girl. I actually hired her to be an intern on my show, and she turned out to be one of the most hardworking young people I've ever met. She is smart and gracious, and at the age of sixteen has more sense and manners than people three times her age. Do you know that she is one of only two people who have ever sent me a handwritten thank-you card? She will work forever, and I'd hire her again in a heartbeat.

I also get along with Michael, Nicole's husband. It wasn't always like that. There were moments during the custody fight when Michael and I almost came to blows.

But he has thanked me for the opportunity I gave his daughter to work in radio. And I've thanked him for all that he's done for Brandon. He's been a kind, supportive father figure all these years, a member of the village that helped to raise my oldest son. I respect that.

Sometimes Malik, my youngest son, goes to visit Brandon, and Brandon's mother and stepfather treat Malik just like family, because, after all, he is. Now everybody's working together in the best interest of all of our children.

I'm still not sure what motivated Nicole to say that Brandon wasn't my son all those years ago. Once she found out that he was, I still don't know why she fought so hard to keep me from playing a role in his life. But now I'm willing to give her the benefit of the doubt. She was sixteen years old, having a baby. And I was young, too, trying to get my bearings. Maybe she felt that Michael was the more solid choice, the guy who could be a more stable father. I don't know, and at this point, it doesn't really matter.

But I will tell you this: I am pro-dad because I am pro-child.

People need to know that fathers are important. There are plenty of good dads out there who don't get the recognition or respect that they deserve. The part they have to play in their children's lives is unmistakable. It's also irreplaceable.

I want to encourage the dads who've gone absent to reassume their rightful place. I want to encourage them not to wait until their children are grown and successful to sweep in, because that's too late. Be there from the start and help guide your sons and daughters all along their way.

I'm thinking of making an acknowledgment of fathers a regular segment on my show, because men coach, teach, and guide children who may not be biologically their own every day, and that is worth celebrating.

IT TAKES A VILLAGE

The moment that I was born, I hit the jackpot. I had seven uncles who taught me to how to dress with class and walk with power. I had the gift of actually knowing my great-grandmothers, sitting on their laps, and listening to their stories. I spent as much time in the homes of my grandparents as I did with my mother. I had all the family anyone could ever hope for, and all the family you could ever need.

Still, you can never have too many people looking out for you. You can never have too much love. To nurture and raise a child, it takes a whole village.

My grandmother Ada only had a fourth-grade education. As smart and wise as she was, she couldn't help me much when it came to knowing the correct way to conjugate a verb. But I had Miss Avery, my sixth-grade teacher at Anna Stuart Dupuy Elementary School. The kids in our class were told that we were slow learners. But by the end of that year, every one of us could add figures and recite the details of history as well as the so-called smart kids down the hall.

In the Kingston Projects, where I grew up, and on the tree-shaded block where my grandparents Ernest and Mattie lived, there were dozens of neighborhood elders. They would warn me off of a rickety fence before I got hurt and tell me to take my behind home if I was still running around after dark. It didn't matter to them that I wasn't their child. The boys and girls in the neighborhood were everybody's children.

There are some kids who need the village much more than others, because the family that they were born into doesn't have the stability, the money, or the strength to build them up. But even kids as fortunate as I was need guidance when their parents aren't standing there beside them. They need someone to fill the gaps in knowledge that their families may not be able to provide. They need guardians all along the way, to help them navigate the unexpected twists, sharp turns, and dead ends that pop up in life.

I THINK BECAUSE so many elders held me close, it was natural for me to feel that same impulse. I believed that I needed to look out for those who were more vulnerable than I was, even when I was still a kid myself. That was the right thing. It was the only thing. I'd experienced that community spirit all of my life.

When I was about eighteen years old, I tried to sign up to be a mentor in the Big Brothers Big Sisters program in Birmingham. I wasn't doing comedy yet. I was stitching together a bunch of different part-time jobs, baking pies at ShowBiz Pizza, selling sneakers at Foot Locker, and playing piano at churches around town. Those small paychecks weren't enough to pay for car insurance, so the Big Brothers Big Sisters program turned me down. But that ended up being okay. Right outside my door, I found plenty of little brothers who needed me.

My mother and I had moved out of the projects and into a nearby apartment complex that everybody called the Bricks. It was the late 1980s, and crack had come along and stomped weed's behind. It was creeping into people's homes, poking into schoolyards, and setting up camp on the corner. It was also creating a whole generation of ne-glected kids, hungry for attention, hungry for comfort, and just plain hungry.

There were two little boys in my complex named Bryce and Harlan whom I used to see outside pretty much every afternoon. They were about five or six years old, and they were always playing ball or pre-tending to be Ninja Turtles or some other character in a comic book or action film. Bryce was brown skinned with big eyes, and Harlan had a deep chocolate complexion and curly dark hair with a little braid dan-gling against his neck.

These kids had close to nothing. You could look at their clothes—pants that were too tight or too short, shirts that were faded and frayed—and see that they were struggling. Bryce had both of his par-ents at home, but they were strung out on crack cocaine. And Harlan was just poor. He lived with his mother and a bunch of other relatives in a small two-bedroom apartment.

They never asked for food, but you could look at these two skinny kids running around outside, and you just knew that they were proba-bly hungry. There was no way I could go home, click on the television, and sit down to dinner knowing that these little boys might be going to bed without anything to eat. And they weren't the only ones in the complex that I worried about.

I started picking up a couple of ham sandwiches and small bags of potato chips on my way home from work. When I'd pull up to the com-plex and see Harlan and Bryce playing, I'd call them over and give them the snacks.

Harlan was particularly shy. But both kids knew me well enough to always wave and say hello, and they were happy to see those sand-wiches and chips. I'm pretty sure that many nights, it was the only din-ner they had.

After a while, I could hardly park my car before Bryce and Harlan were running over, smiling and gazing into my windows. They were happy to see me and probably even more excited to see what I'd brought them.

Other kids in the complex began to notice and would join Bryce and Harlan coming up to my car. I started going to the supermarket, buying packs of wieners and loaves of bread, and cooking when I got home. I'd chop up those hot dogs, skewer them with toothpicks, pull out bottles of ketchup and mustard, and invite the neighborhood kids inside to have an after-school treat.

When I worked at ShowBiz Pizza, if someone called in an order but didn't pick it up, the manager would let one of the employees take the pie home. I started making extra pizzas on purpose. When no one claimed them, I'd take them back to the complex and give all the kids a slice.

I was feeding as many kids as I could, but I grew particularly close to Bryce and Harlan. Their families had gotten to know and trust me, so before long, they would let me take them for ice cream or bring them to work. I would drum up a few tokens so that they could play video games while I was baking pizzas or manning the cash register on the evening shift. They'd spend the time zapping digital bad guys and munching on pizza.

I also started buying both boys things that they needed when I got paid, like a new pair of socks when I noticed the ones they were wearing were gray and dangling around their ankles, or new sneakers when I saw theirs had been run into the ground.

Both kids loved to hang around me, but the truth was that Harlan needed me more. Bryce would go places with us a couple of times a week, but Harlan was with me practically every day. It got to the point that I was listed as an emergency contact for Harlan at his school.

One day, my phone rang and it was Harlan's teacher. My heart started pounding when she told me who she was. Harlan was a sweet, quiet kid. Had someone beaten him up?

It turned out that while Harlan was sitting in class, a cockroach had crawled out of his backpack. It was just one more thing for the kids to tease him about, along with his shabby clothes and shaggy, curly Afro. My heart slowed down when I realized that he was physically okay, but it hurt to think about how humiliated he must have been. I bought him a new backpack and a can of bug spray so that he could try to bug-proof his things at home.

I knew experiences like that bug crawling out of his bag in front of his schoolmates were knocking down Harlan's already low self-esteem. I was determined to do everything I could to help him feel better.

I started taking him to the barber every few weeks to get his hair cut. It was more like an outing than a chore. In the black community, the hair salon and the barbershop are like the town square. You walk in, sit in a chair underneath the Barack Obama posters and notices about a fraternity's next gala, and laugh and gossip about politics and whatever else is going on in the community. You walk out of there feeling nourished and looking fresh. Even as a little boy, Harlan looked forward to going.

But one particular Saturday, we both saw someone at the shop who knocked the wind out of us. It was Harlan's father.

I knew who he was. He lived right there in Birmingham, but he didn't give one thin dime to Harlan's mother and barely saw his young son. To make matters worse, he had the nerve to be sitting in the shop with another kid. I have no idea who the child was, but it damn sure wasn't Harlan, and it should have been.

We both ignored him. Harlan got his hair clipped, and we said our goodbyes to Tony, the barber, and some of the other clients. We headed toward the door. But Harlan's father, who hadn't said a word to us in the shop, had the nerve to get up and follow us outside.

"Hey, man," he mumbled as Harlan walked ahead of us, toward my car. "Thanks for everything you're doing for Harlan."

I didn't want to make a big scene in front of Harlan. I'm sure the scene inside the shop was painful enough. So I kept that conversation short. I said that Harlan was a great kid, he needed a haircut, and I was doing what I could. I turned away and kept it moving.

Inside, I was steaming. I didn't have enough money to get my own hair cut. I was walking around with a bumpy Afro, spending the little cash I earned to make sure that Harlan looked good, so that he might feel better about himself and not get teased at school. But I didn't have time to ask Harlan's father why he didn't take better care of his child. I didn't have time to lecture him on what I'm sure he already knew that he should have been doing. I represented the village, and I needed to keep my energy and focus on Harlan.

A couple of years later, when I moved out of my mother's apartment and got my own place, I continued to stay in Harlan's life. He would call me up on a Friday asking if he could spend the night, and I'd drop whatever I was doing to go pick him up.

One weekend there was a bad storm. The lightning was lighting up the whole apartment, and the thunder sounded like a train roaring right up to the front door. I'd turned one of the two bedrooms into a small den with a couch, and that's where Harlan, who was eight years old at the time, slept.

I was lying in my room when the thunder and lightning woke me up. I bet myself that it would be about five minutes before Harlan came running into my room. It took less time than that. I closed my eyes; heard another thunderclap, followed by some footsteps; and then boom—Harlan was standing next to my bed, looking pitiful and petrified.

"Are you scared?" I asked, like I didn't already know. He just nodded his head. I told him that he could stay in my room. I made a pallet on the floor for myself and let him stay in my bed. He jumped under the covers and fell fast asleep.

It doesn't take a lot to know when a child needs you. Sometimes it's common sense, like when a storm sounds like it's about to take the roof off. Other times, it's just keeping your eyes open or being a good listener. You see a little boy being teased, a little girl who's poorly dressed, a teenager who's gravitating toward a rowdy crowd, and you step in and try to do what you can to make the situation better.

You can ask the kids doing the teasing how they would feel if the shoe were on the other foot. If you have a couple of dollars, you can buy that underdressed kid a coat. You can drop off a bag of groceries at a struggling child's house.

I learned sitting in the pews of New Mt. Olive Church, in the halls of Anna Stuart Dupuy Elementary, and in the living rooms of my grandparents and their neighbors that you could make a child's day or change a child's life just by paying a little attention and getting involved.

Harlan is now thirty-two years old, and the love and respect that we have for each other is still strong.

Not long ago, I called him and Bryce. I said that I wanted to connect with both of them in a few days, so that we could speak to some kids about the power of mentoring. But I actually had a surprise. When they showed up at my house, we drove to the airport and flew on a private plane to Cincinnati, where I did a show with Katt Williams. Harlan and Bryce were my special guests, with front-row seats, and afterward, we hung out backstage, took a whole bunch of pictures, and just had a great time.

Harlan has a good job with Federal Express. He's married and is a wonderful father to his two children. He was always a kind kid, and so there's a chance that he would have turned out to be a great father and husband all on his own. He also could have become a mirror of his own father, who ignored him.

But the village had stepped in. And I'm not just talking about me. I'm talking about the teacher who picked up the phone to let me know that a bug had crawled out of his bag, that he'd had a bad day and he needed support. And I'm sure that there were others along the way who took a positive interest in the life of a needy little boy.

Harlan grew up to be the kind of man any of us would want our children to be. And so did Bryce, who is a truck driver with a lovely wife and three great kids. I can't tell you how good it feels to look at Harlan and Bryce and know that I played a role in helping mentor these hardworking, generous, and kindhearted men who are now passing along their love and gifts to the next generation.

I'VE HELPED TO create two children, my biological sons, Brandon and Malik. But I've helped raise a whole tribe.

My best friend at Miles College was a guy named Terrence West. Everybody called him T. West. He was tall, with his hair clipped into a short cut, and the ladies loved him. After we both pledged Omega Psi Phi, we'd go to parties and chat up the honeys side by side. And we stomped together at the step shows, the dance competitions that pitted us against the members of the other major black fraternities—Phi Beta Sigma, Alpha Phi Alpha, and the cane-tossing brothers of Kappa Alpha Psi.

"Q Psi Phi!!!"

Frat or no frat, T. and I were brothers. He was there for me as I fell in and out of love, and I was there when he had his two little boys, Terrell and T. J. He was never so happy as he was when they were born.

We would drive all the way to Tuscaloosa to get some Dreamland barbecue, washing down those juicy ribs and spicy baked beans with big glasses of sweet tea. We would blast the music and laugh the entire distance there and back, 116 miles each way. Then one day, T. was gone. Police found him tied up in the backseat of his car, with his wallet missing. He'd been shot to death and robbed. My friend was dead, and suddenly his sons became mine.

Terrell's mother, Angel, and T. J.'s mom, Telisha, were generous from the start, always welcoming me to share in the boys' lives. Terrell and T. J. would stay with me most weekends and then for entire summers. I knew what they were going through. I had lost my father at a young age, too. The only reason that void didn't become a bottomless pit inside me was because I had so many father figures—my uncles, grandfather, and coaches—who were there to fill it with love and encouragement instead. I tried to do the same for Terrell and T. J.

Thanks to the hard work T. put in before he died, and all the love and support the boys continued to get from their mothers and the relatives and friends who surrounded them, both T. J. and Terrell were unbelievably grounded from the time they were very young. If you let your kids have a party, T. J. and Terrell were the kids you'd want to leave in charge. They'd make sure nothing got out of hand and tell a troublemaker to cut it out in a minute, and if they needed backup, they wouldn't hesitate to get you or another adult to set things right.

Terrell is now a student and running back at Middle Tennessee

State University. And T. J. is attending Miles College in Birmingham. Those boys are now men, and they continue to make me proud.

Then there are my girls. D'essence was about two years old when I began dating her mother, Elizabeth. I remember the first time I saw D'essence. She was sitting in her car seat, and when I approached the window, she turned and reached out to me. It was like she recognized who I was, like she had been waiting for me. She seemed to know that I would be her daddy.

Elizabeth and I had a son together, Malik. Ultimately, our relationship didn't last, but between Malik and D'essence, who was basically my daughter, we were forever a family. Like Terrell and T. J., D'essence was with me most weekends, and since I lived near some of the best schools in Alabama, she eventually lived with me full-time. Just the other day, I was looking at a picture of myself taking her to kindergarten on the first day. I would pick her up every afternoon, and she'd talk my ear off about the monkeys she'd read about, the pictures she'd drawn, and the games she'd played at recess, until I finally had to tell her to zip it. She'd make a motion like she was zipping her lips and throwing away the key, and then it would be peace and quiet in my truck all the rest of the way home.

Aaryn came into my life in much the same way.

I met Aaryn's mother, Tamika, when I was performing in Indianapolis. After the show, Mike Epps and I were standing in the lobby, selling T-shirts, and she walked up. She was pretty and sexy. I glimpsed her little Alpha Kappa Alpha key chain and started rapping.

"What's up, Slim?" I said. And we soon started dating.

She had a two-year-old daughter, Aaryn, and since Malik and Aaryn were the same age, I started calling them my twins. When Tamika and I were no longer romantically involved, it was clear that neither she nor Aaryn was going anywhere. I loved Aaryn, and Tamika loved D'essence, Brandon, and Malik.

Aaryn's father wasn't providing financial support to help care for her, and I saw Tamika jumping through hoops that she shouldn't have had to. Finally one day, I asked Tamika to tell that fool to sign over his parental rights, so she and I could officially raise Aaryn together. Biology isn't worth a damn if you don't take care of your responsibilities. She told me that wasn't necessary, but I kept pressing. Aaryn was a sweet kid, and she needed and deserved a full-time dad.

I started giving Tamika money every month, not because she asked, but because I wanted to. If Aaryn needed a barrette, pink Lustrasilk hair moisturizer, Fruit Roll-Ups, or coloring books, I was going to make sure she had them, and anything else that she needed.

When Aaryn got a little older, she was on a plane to visit me in Birmingham every other weekend. Now, I'm not saying that Aaryn's mother and I never clashed. When you are involved with someone romantically, and things don't work out, the personality differences that broke you up don't just disappear. We would sometimes argue about petty stuff. But no argument ever overshadowed our dedication to taking care of and supporting all of our children.

Our co-parenting arrangement is simply awesome. Tamika will help counsel me when I'm having some trouble with Malik or any of the other kids, not just her biological daughter, Aaryn. We spend some Thanksgivings and Christmases all together. And in the past, when I've gone out of town for a few days to perform, Tamika has stayed at my house with all of the children—my son with Elizabeth, Malik; Elizabeth's daughter, D'essence; Tamika's daughter, Aaryn; and the son I had with Nicole, my high school girlfriend, Brandon. Each of our children belongs to both of us.

Tamika recently got a great opportunity with the oil company she works for to move to Bogotá, Colombia, and Aaryn went with her, to spend time with her mom and to take advantage of a potentially once-in-a-lifetime experience to live overseas. But Aaryn comes home to visit often.

As a matter of fact, she was just here for spring break. From the yard, I could see she had turned on the bathroom light, the closet light, and the light in the ceiling fan, wasting electricity and money. But she is the best, smartest, most well-spoken kid. She wants to be a doctor and doesn't really do anything but study and read—which is why I guess she needs every light in the house to be on.

She's all about making the most of her education. One of the best choices I ever made in my life was my decision to father her. I'm so glad that her mother and I were able to see the big picture, the need to come together to provide a strong foundation, so that all of our children could grow into confident adults who know how to be in this world and who will hopefully pass on what we give them to another generation.

I appreciate Tamika and Telisha, Angel and Elizabeth, and also Candace, the mother of my adopted nephew and niece, Craig and Jurnee. They were all generous enough to allow me to be a part of their children's lives, and their openness was critical because a village can't take shape if some of the villagers lock their doors and shut the rest out. There has to be unity. It's like when a sewing circle comes to-gether to stitch a quilt. They are able to get so much done, so much more quickly, by harnessing all their energy, and the fabric they sew is so strong, it's hard for anyone to tear it apart.

THERE ARE SOME mistakes you might make as a young person that you can't recover from. There are teenagers or people in their twenties who made decisions that resulted in their getting a life sentence or led to their lying in a morgue. But mistakes don't have to be so dire or long lasting as those.

They say, "You'd do better if you knew better." And sometimes young people need the village to teach them those lessons. They might think that they can act out in public, or present themselves any old way, and it won't have any repercussions. But the village can shift them in the right direction, if those of us within it put our arms around our youths instead of putting them down or writing them off.

When I was in high school, after every football game, everybody would gather at the McDonald's on First Avenue in the Woodlawn neighborhood.

There was a police officer who used to moonlight there as a security guard when he was off duty. He was a slim black guy, with curly salt-and-pepper hair. He was very distinguished looking and friendly, the type of officer who kept the kids calm by being strong and present, instead of confrontational and aggressive. That is, until he had to be.

One afternoon when I was in the eleventh grade, I decided that I wanted to cut up a little bit. I was sitting at a table talking loudly and cracking jokes. The more my classmates laughed, the louder I got. But I was disturbing the other customers and getting a little too rowdy.

The officer came over to where I was sitting. "I hear you doing too much," he said. "You need to calm down."

But I was feeling myself at that point, getting attention, commanding the crowd. I just kept on going.

Before I could pop out my next joke, that cop had grabbed me by the back of my shirt, pulled me to the side of the restaurant, and pushed me against the wall, not hard enough to hurt me, but hard enough for me to get the message.

"You're in a public place," he said, getting close to my face. "You need to respect yourself and respect the people around you. And if a police officer tells you to cut it out, you need to do it." Then he let me go.

Of course, I was embarrassed. I slunk back to where I'd been sitting, told my friends that everything was all right, and plopped my butt down. Comedy hour was over.

At the time, I resented what that officer did. But I never forgot it. And when I see him around town now, as I often do, thirty years later, I say thank you and give him a hug—every single time.

I thank him for getting me together. He didn't have to do that. He could have said nothing at all. Then, the next time I was in a restaurant, or at the park, or riding on the bus, I could have started cutting up again, being loud and brash because I didn't expect any bad consequences. And the next police officer I ran into might not have been so nice, and I could have wound up being taken to jail.

I needed someone to talk to me. I needed someone to care. My mother and grandparents were at work or at home. My uncles weren't nearby. But that officer was.

One night not long ago, I was performing at one of the local comedy clubs, and I spotted him in the audience. I stopped my act and pointed him out. "How are you doing, man?" I asked. "You know I love you, right?" He looked so proud, nodding his head. I invited him and his wife backstage and embraced them both.

I try to pass along the same kind of care and attention that I received from that police officer and so many others.

For instance, too often I see young men walking down the street with their pants sagging and their underwear peeking out. I don't roll my eyes or judge the parents who let them out of the house looking like that. Instead, I pull those young men to the side and say, "Let me talk to you."

Often, they recognize me. "Oh man," they say, smiling and shaking my hand. "Rickey Smiley! What's up?"

I don't waste time grinning and making nice. "Do you know that somebody walking behind you could be the one to give you an opportunity that could change your life? There could be somebody you strike up a conversation with who might give you a chance to make some money and take your life to a whole other level."

Then I come in with the kicker. "And do you know why you're going to miss that opportunity? Because they're walking behind you, looking at your underwear. You only have one chance to make a first impression. Young man, where is your belt?"

Usually they start stuttering, fumbling for an answer. I cut them off.

"Here you go," I say. "Take mine. And put it on. Right now."

I am serious. I have given away probably one hundred belts.

Some people might worry that if they said that to one of these teenagers walking around, they'd get cursed out or worse. But I have never had a problem. Every single young man I've spoken to has respected me enough to put that belt on. I shake their hands and send them on their own way, with a new belt and hopefully a new perspective on how to present themselves to the world.

One time, I was riding up the escalator at Hartsfield-Jackson Atlanta International Airport. There was a young man, about six foot four, wearing a University of Texas jacket standing in front of me. And his underwear was in my face for the entire ride.

When we stepped off, I approached him. "What's up, man?" I said. "I'm Rickey Smiley."

"Hey. How you doing?" he said, smiling.

"That's a nice jacket. Do you play college basketball?"

"Yes, sir, University of Texas," he said with pride.

"So that's a longhorn on your back?" I said, referring to the school's mascot.

"Absolutely," he said, sticking his chest out a little.

"Let me ask you a question," I said. "Why are you walking around showing off your underwear when you're representing the university?"

"Ah, man," he said, that smile dropping from his face real fast. "That ain't got nothing—"

I revved up. "You are representing the University of Texas. That's where Kevin Durant played. They've won national football championships. All kinds of famous people have graduated from there, and you might one day be one of them. I should never be standing behind you, seeing that you are a student and athlete at that school, and have to look at your underwear, because that doesn't match what you're representing."

He paused for a second. Then he apologized, shook my hand, and gave me a big hug. He also thanked me for the belt I pulled off my waist so that he could hike up his Levi's.

Now, I could have said, "Tsk, tsk. That's a damn shame. Look at him," and kept on walking to my flight. But I didn't write him off. I taught. I cared.

Because each of our children is all of our children, their business is my business. I want them to have all the opportunities that life can give them. I'm trying to let them know, here's some advice for you, here's something that you can use. I hope you take it and run with it.

———————

SOMETIMES, THE VILLAGE can only do so much. You have to want to be guided. You have to want to be fathered.

My nephew Craig lived with me for several years, but we reached a point where he wasn't willing to respect my rules. He was throwing parties and skipping school. I put him out in the garage for a while, and even paddled him a few times, like when he didn't show up for class and then tried to fool me by getting back to school in time to hop the bus and get dropped off at the house.

But his behavior wasn't improving, and so when he decided that he wanted to move in with his grandmother, I gladly let him go. I slept well every night knowing I had done what I was supposed to do. As a matter of fact, I slept much better than I had in a while, because I didn't have to lie there with one eye open, worrying about his stealing his cousin's phone or sneaking out.

There are too many other kids out there who want to be raised, who want to be given guidance, to keep on trying to steer someone who's grown and rejecting what you have to offer. You can have coaches, but it doesn't do much good if you aren't willing to listen to them, to take what they teach and apply it to your game. It's the same with life.

I had a lot of difficulties with the mother of my oldest son, Brandon, which was one of the two biggest disappointments in my life. The other was what I went through with another one of my children who wasn't biologically mine, but whom I'd raised just the same.

The interesting thing is one experience led to the other. When I sought a paternity test to determine if I was Brandon's father, I became friendly with one of the women working for my attorney at the time.

Her name was Lorraine. One day, she brought her young daughter Melody to work. Lorraine, who had seen me with Brandon and obviously knew that I was fighting to be in his life, told me that Melody's father wasn't around. I told her that I would be happy to have Melody hang out with me and Brandon sometimes.

I had started doing comedy by then, and I was living in a town house. Melody would come over, and she, Brandon, and I would all jump on the trampoline together, ride bikes, and bake 7-Up cakes. Pretty quickly, Melody became like my daughter. I used to even dress her and Brandon in matching colors.

I had a major role in raising Melody over the next ten years. I taught her how to cook smothered chicken and black-eyed peas. I went to her basketball games. And since I wasn't her father, I signed some paperwork that I believed would make it simpler to get medical care for Melody if it was ever needed while she was staying or traveling with me. Unfortunately, I didn't realize those papers stated that I was Melody's dad. I was no longer represented by my previous attorney, but if I had been thinking, I would have hired someone else to look over those documents.

Everything was good until around the time Melody turned sixteen. That's when her mother decided to snatch her out of my life.

I'd never had a romantic relationship with Lorraine, Melody's mom. I volunteered to help raise Melody, provided for her financially, and sometimes had her live with me and my other children when I absolutely did not have to. But instead of being appreciative, Lorraine took that paperwork I had signed years before and got an order for a staggering amount in back and future child support.

I never received notice that I was supposed to show up in court. I only learned about it when I was served another document—a warrant for my arrest based on my failure to appear.

I ended up sitting in jail in Walker County, a highly conservative pocket of Alabama with a reputation for being hard on African-Americans. To anybody looking at the situation, the chance that a judge would rule in favor of a black man accused of denying child support to Melody's mom, who happened to be a single white mother, was little to none. But I was determined to fight.

I posted bail and hired an attorney. He figured that Lorraine would be satisfied with a little cash and that I should just give her $5,000 to make her go away. But I refused. It wasn't about the money, it was the principle.

That case took years to resolve. But in the end, I won and didn't have to pay Lorraine one penny—though I'd certainly paid a whole lot in legal fees.

That whole terrible scenario made me think about how I needed to live according to the way that my grandfather had taught me to drive up to a red light. You don't race up to it. You have to slow down and take stock of the situation. You have to evaluate what's visible around you, and also peek into the shadows to see what isn't so clear.

There was nothing wrong with wanting to bring Melody into my family. She was a little girl who needed a father figure. But I should have paused and investigated the situation further. I should have slowed down and carefully read that paperwork her mother brought to me to sign and withheld my signature until I thoroughly understood it. Not taking that time cost me years of my life, and a mountain of lawyer fees.

Still, Lorraine's greed and selfishness, as awful as they were, were not what made this experience so painful. It was the way Melody behaved that really stung.

Melody virtually stopped coming around, even when she was on her own and able to do what she wanted without her mother's say-so. And right after *Rickey Smiley for Real*, my reality show on TV One, debuted, Melody started trashing me on social media.

I never rejected Melody. She had rejected me. And not just me, but the other kids, T. J. and Terrell, Malik and Aaryn, D'essence and Brandon, Craig and Jurnee. She stopped talking to them, cut them off completely, even though they had loved and embraced her as a sister.

I would have liked for our relationship to have stayed strong. I considered her my child. But sometimes, when God removes certain people from your life, it's a blessing. You have to ask yourself if you're better off. Melody was fathered. She was mentored. She was loved. You do what you can for the young people of the village, and then they have to grow up and make their own decisions. You just try to do your best, and then it's up to them what comes next.

I had other kids to raise, other kids to worry about. There's a young lady I put through college who's about to get her doctorate. My niece Porshé graduated from Clark College, and her sister, ReeRee, just married a wonderful, hardworking young man, and the two of them have their own business.

God moved aside someone who didn't care about what I had to give so I could continue focusing on fathering, shepherding, and guiding other young people who did.

You aren't going to have all of the blessings that I've been given and not go through some hardships. More importantly, no matter who you are or what you've done, things don't always go smoothly in life. But you have to continue trying to do what you think is right.

Think about how many planes experience turbulence. It happens almost every flight. But how often do you hear about a plane crashing because of it? Now, if the pilot put on the brakes as soon as it hit those air pockets, the plane would plunge to the ground. Instead, it's got to keep going, and before long, it hits an area of calm.

The experience with Melody was disappointing, but it didn't make me bitter. It didn't make me turn my back on other kids in need. I couldn't stop. And I had to trust that in the end, it would work out as it should.

We are born to serve. If you're willing to give your last, you'll get it back double. But that's not the reason you do it. It's not about you. You do it because giving is right, because each of us has gifts worth sharing that can strengthen our families, our neighborhoods, our larger communities.

And who is more deserving than each of our children? Who is more deserving than all of our children?

It's easy to complain about that kid from around the corner who robbed Miss Carter. But did you ever offer him a meal when he was younger and you saw him wandering around, doing without? It's easy to shake your finger about those kids who've drifted away from the church, but do you volunteer for programs that might draw them in?

Being part of the village isn't easy, but it's necessary. Some of those young people you try to reach may not listen. Some may reject you. Some may benefit from what you gave them and never say thank you.

But then, some of them will.

I was walking through my old neighborhood one day when a woman approached me.

"Mr. Smiley," she said, stopping me in my tracks. "Do you remember me? When I was in middle school, you took me and some other kids up to Central Plaza, and you bought me my first bicycle. You were driving a green Jeep Cherokee . . . Thank you."

I didn't remember doing that, but it sounded like something that I would have done. And I am glad that I did it.

YOU ARE NOT A CHICKEN: BREAKING OUT OF YOUR COMFORT ZONE

Sometimes, you have to get out of your own way to let God's blessings come in.

I know that we are all dedicated and loyal to our cousins and some of the boys and girls we played with on the block, but sometimes those connections can stunt your growth. What's meant for you isn't necessarily meant for Pookie; Cousin Robert Earl; or Jamie, who used to spend the night with you at your grandmother's house when you were a little kid. Sometimes, you just have to fly solo.

When a space shuttle goes up, those rocket boosters on its sides eventually separate from the shuttle and drop back to earth, so that the shuttle can go into orbit. Just like that spacecraft, sometimes you also have to shed dead weight so you can soar. You're not obligated to carry along everybody you grew up with, or to be with everyone you meet along the way, for an entire lifetime.

You can get trapped by an old way of thinking and become your own worst enemy. I grew up in the projects, but that didn't mean I had to have a stereotypical project mentality. I'd ride around town with my grandfather, learning how to pay bills. In high school, I was that dude who worked on the golf course, talking to the older black gentlemen lining up at the tees, trying to find out how I could go in a different direction. Walking with them across the sloping green, I picked up career advice right along with those golf balls.

Subsidized housing is a place to live if you can't afford more or better on your own. There's no shame in it, but that environment shouldn't limit you, either. You don't have to be stuck in the "hood," and you don't have to be loyal to it, either. If the folks you know there aren't striving to do something worthwhile with their lives, if they're content in that zone, you've got to leave them behind. It's great if you want to go back from time to time to inspire some of the young people growing up in the old neighborhood, but you can achieve that through a steady stream of visits. It doesn't have to be an everyday thing. Help the kids, but then make sure you keep it moving.

Part of the problem when you're trying to stick with some family members and old friends is that you end up running in place. You're expending energy but getting nowhere. When you're busy trying to fit in, your perspective stays narrow, and you can't see the bigger picture. Or you start to do better than everybody else, and they make you feel guilty. They start whispering that you're getting cocky or forgetting where you came from. Sometimes, especially in your career, you have to surround yourself with people who are doing better than you, because that success, that drive, that ambition, rubs off on you. Even if you weren't looking for it, you start to soak it all in.

Have you ever seen a flock of eagles? I'll bet you haven't. Eagles fly alone. They're birds, of course, just like chickens, but you never see those two species hanging out together. And you've never been able to go to Popeyes and buy a four-piece box of eagle. Eagles fly too high; you can't catch them and turn them into lunch. *That's* how you have to live. You've got to be like an eagle: bold enough to separate from the flock, courageous enough to get off the ground and fly solo.

If you don't relate to birds, think about fish. They are confined, swimming around in a small fishbowl or tank. But if you toss a fish into a pond, that fish may experience a little shock. It may be uncomfortable or even afraid, but that fish now has the opportunity to grow. It's the same for you and me. You leave behind the familiar—your old neighborhood, that job you've worked for what seems like forever, that romantic relationship that's become like poison—and it may be a challenge, it may be scary, it may be uncomfortable. But you'll grow.

In 1992, I got a big break on television when I started appearing on HBO's *Def Comedy Jam*. It was a showcase that had been launched by the rap music mogul Russell Simmons, and some of the greatest black comedians at the time appeared on it. I'm talking about Chris Rock, Mike Epps, and Bill Bellamy, to name just a few.

The show had come to Birmingham to scout talent, and I decided to try to get a meeting with its creative team. I remember that I was sitting in the lobby of the building where they were holding auditions, clutching a videocassette that contained clips of my comedy routines, when Bill Bellamy walked by.

Bellamy was a television host and a video jockey (and eventually he went on to be a movie star in films like *Any Given Sunday* and *Love Jones*). It was exciting to see him, and I jumped at the opportunity to meet him.

"Hi. I'm Rickey Smiley," I said, rising from my seat and reaching out to shake his hand. "I'm a comedian from Birmingham." Bill said hello, then looked at the tape I was holding in my hand, then back again at me.

"As long as you're funny," he said, "they're going to book you." He offered to take the tape in to the producer personally. A few days later, I found out that I'd gotten the gig, and soon after, I started touring colleges and performing in front of hundreds of students week after week.

Before you knew it, I was able to quit my jobs—*all* of them. I had been selling shoes at Foot Locker, selling equipment at Hibbett Sports, and playing the piano at one church and the organ at another. Now I was able to focus totally on comedy.

Def Comedy Jam was a springboard, but it was BET's *Comic View* that really put me on the map. I also started appearing on that show in 1992, eventually going on to host in 2000 and 2004. But even though I was developing this national profile, I was still in my comfort zone back in Birmingham. I'd first been a comedian featured on the morning drive-time show on 95.7 FM. Then I'd appeared on the Doug Banks radio show, which was syndicated. My characters and prank calls were growing my fan base. I bought a nice house, I was raising my son Brandon after finally winning custody, and I headed to my grandmother's house for dinner every Sunday after church. I was flying, but I was landing back in the same roost where I'd always been.

Sometimes, though, God makes you uncomfortable so you can soar.

In 2006, my grandmother Mattie died. I was her baby. I remember when I was a little boy, walking out of the apartment where I lived with my mother and seeing my grandmother waiting at the corner to take me to her and my grandfather's house. Imagining life without her made me feel like I was drifting, like I'd lost my anchor. Then, a few days after she'd passed away, the phone rang. It was Steve Harvey.

Steve was on the air in Dallas, but he was leaving the show. The Radio One executives who owned the station had asked who should replace him, and he gave them my name.

"You need to come to Dallas and get on this radio," Steve said.

"Well," I told him, hesitating, "I don't know. I just bought a house . . ."

"Yeah, well how are you gonna pay for that house?" Steve said back.

"Well, I do stand-up . . ."

That was it. Steve called me a fool—well, he called me more than that—and slammed down the phone.

A couple of minutes later, the phone rang again. This time it was Boomerang. That's Steve's bodyguard. He's like my big brother—a really large, scary, no-nonsense big brother.

"You ungrateful son of a b----. If you don't get on that m-----f------ plane, we ain't never gonna f--- with you again!" Then *he* hung up on me.

I didn't know *what* to do. I talked to my grandfather about everything, but he didn't really know the world of stand-up comedy or radio. I think ultimately it was the replay in my mind of Boomerang's voice cursing me out that pushed me to take that job. It took me back to my peewee football days, playing for the Tarrant Wildcats, when the coaches would tell me to pull my butt off the ground and get back in the game. That's what Boomerang and Steve were saying: "Get your a-- on a plane, and get down here and do this job!"

My attorney and I arranged a call with Alfred Liggins, the CEO of Radio One, and negotiated a salary along with some other details, and two weeks later, I was on a plane again. The plan was that I would fly to Dallas every Sunday, stay in town until Thursday, and then do the show Friday from Birmingham. Though I was able to do the show from my hometown once a week, I needed to be in Dallas the rest of the time because if you're going to win on radio, you need to have a local presence. Listeners need to be able to see you out and about, to know that you are a part of their community.

But where was I going to go to Bible study? Who was I going to have dinner with when I was done with work and wanted some company? After fighting so hard to get my son, how often was I going to get to see him, since I would be in Texas much of the week? I won't lie. I teared up during that flight, because I was so far out of my comfort zone and overwhelmed.

For all those reasons, it was important for me to pick up and move to Dallas. It was challenging. It was uncomfortable. It was frightening. But I grew. I was able to build a brand from that one simple business decision. I had to get out of Birmingham, take a chance, and trust God.

Once I was on the ground in Dallas, I knew that I had to jump fully into my new life. I started asking people about a local church led by a pastor who was engaged in civil rights. I found Friendship-West Baptist Church, which had a powerful minister, Dr. Frederick Douglass Haynes. I went down to Friendship-West on the first Sunday that I could. I started making some friends, volunteered for activities, and connected with a lady who I swore looked just like my beloved grandmother Mattie. I didn't sit around talking about Birmingham. I took on the culture of Dallas. I grew.

I started having Pastor Haynes on my new show. Some folks warned me that he was already appearing on a program hosted by one of my competitors, and others warned him that the competing station wouldn't like it. But Pastor Haynes saw the big picture. He wasn't scared to fly solo. He followed his own advice and tuned out the noise from the crowd. As it turns out, my show became the number one hip-hop program in the market, and then we got syndicated, airing on stations around the country. So Pastor Haynes is now on the radio with me in eighty cities. He increased his visibility, and he was able to spread his message farther, by making the right decision—by being an eagle, not a chicken.

That call from Steve just days after I lost my grandmother was, I feel, God's way of giving me something else to focus on. It forced me to stretch beyond what was familiar. I was already a Dallas Cowboys fan, and the people of Dallas really embraced me. I turned around and did the same to them. They'd never had anybody in Dallas speak the way that I did on the radio, about civil rights, about social injustice. Listeners were asking, "Where the hell did you come from?"

I strove to be no-nonsense and bold. I said what needed to be said, and I called out anybody who I felt was doing wrong. That's how I began fighting, and rallying others to fight with me, to free Shaquanda Cotton.

Shaquanda was a fourteen-year-old girl who lived in Paris, Texas. She allegedly shoved a teacher's aide who was working as a hall attendant, who Shaquanda said was preventing her from going to the nurse's office to get her medication. Shaquanda was arrested and had been in jail for nearly a year when I learned about her situation. She grew so despondent that some news reports said that she began to contemplate committing suicide.

When I heard about the case from an activist who appeared on my show, I talked about the injustice of it on the air nearly every day. To me, it was just another example of how black boys and girls were more harshly disciplined for the most minor offenses. Finally, I worked with a group of local residents committed to the fight for social justice to organize a protest in Shaquanda's hometown. We surrounded the courthouse, held up placards, and made speeches calling for Shaquanda's release. Soon after, the governor sent word to let that child out of jail.

So what are you going to be? An eagle or a chicken?

You have to get out of your own way. People who live in Dallas need to move to Atlanta. People in Atlanta need to move to Miami. You get my point. You don't have to actually move to a different city, but you do need to get up and move *somewhere*—to a new social situation, to a new job track, to a new relationship—so you can begin to think more broadly and see more clearly.

I was in my comfort zone in Alabama, but when my grandmother died and I got the call from Steve offering me a new job on his old station, I picked up and went to Dallas. I was used to going to my grandmother's house every Sunday for dinner. I was used to living in Birmingham, where I knew every street, where I knew every neighborhood, and where it seemed I was acquainted with almost every person. What was I going to do in Dallas?

But the answer was, I was going to grow—in a way that I never would have if I had just stayed in Birmingham. If I had been loyal to just one city, if I had just wanted to stay comfortable, my radio career would have stopped with the Doug Banks show—a platform that reflected the vision and priorities of somebody else. It was uncomfortable to leave my son and my family and to not know where I was going to go to church. But the way my business, my world, and my life expanded made all the discomfort worth it. I want to inspire everyone to burst out of their cocoon and try something new. Get away from the chickens.

I haven't just left cities behind. I've also had to cut loose people, some of whom I loved, who just didn't fit in my life anymore.

I'm a member of Omega Psi Phi, and I bleed the fraternity's colors of Royal Purple and Old Gold. It's one of the original African-American fraternities, founded on November 17, 1911, at Howard University, and its members have included Dr. Charles Drew; Washington, DC, kingmaker Vernon Jordan; the great poet Langston Hughes; and basketball star Vince Carter. But every brother isn't a friend, and every friend isn't a brother. I don't automatically trust or hang out with someone just because he knows the fraternity handshake.

I'm telling you that you don't have to go to your once-in-a-decade class reunion if you think you'll feel uncomfortable. And if you have aunts, uncles, or other extended family members who say you can't succeed or that you're dreaming too big, you don't have to go to all your family functions, either. Sometimes, you may even have to declare your independence from a parent who says you cannot make it.

Now, I can't emphasize enough how important it is to honor your mother and father. Without them, none of us would be here. The day you were born, they gave you the greatest gift they could, and hopefully, they'll give you even more throughout your life. But sometimes, even your own mother or father may lack vision. They may be limited by their own experiences, weighed down by life's challenges, or just frightened at the thought of your moving far away. You always need to respect them, check on them, and care for them. But once you're grown, you have a right—I would say you have an obligation—to see where your path can take you. You are an eagle.

When you need to make a break from people who are putting you down or stifling your dreams, you don't have to call a meeting with them and make a speech, yelling to the world, "I'm outta here, y'all." You don't have to post a statement on Facebook or send out a group text. All of those loud, public declarations just keep you mired in the mess, the very thing you're trying to get away from. Just make your peace and step off quietly.

I've got a bunch of former employees and an ex-wife who always get together. I call them the Rickey Smiley Recovery Group. You know they must be talking about me like I'm a dog, because they never send me an invitation. I'm the reason they all met in the first place—I was married to one of them, and the rest used to work for me—and I don't ever see an Evite pop up in my inbox. They're all over social media, posting pictures of the clique chowing down at Applebee's or going to one another's houses for parties, and I never learn about the get-togethers until they're all over.

I won't deny that it hurt a little bit when I first realized they were always gathering and that I was being left out. But I get it. They don't like me for whatever reasons, despite what I did for many of them, and I've come to be okay with that. I just try to do the right thing by everybody whom I meet. If you hire somebody to do a job and it's not working out, at some point, you have to let them go. If you are in a romantic relationship that is not working, no matter how hard you've tried, you have to move on, so both of you can try to find some happiness in the years that you have left. And if a group that you were once a part of rejects you, puts you down, or lies about you, you don't have to try to prove your worth to get back in those folks' good graces. You can just silently, quickly, and politely pull away.

It's difficult to face the fact that some people in your circle of acquaintances, coworkers, or relatives may be envious of you. But the sad truth is, sometimes they are. And if you don't get away from that energy, it can bring you down. In the most extreme circumstances, it can even end your life. Look at the Tejano singer Selena, this budding superstar who was shot by a rabid fan to whom she'd given a job. All she did was give somebody an opportunity, and that lady took Selena's life.

What happened to Selena was obviously unusual and extreme. You won't necessarily lose everything to someone who resents you. But they can damage your reputation, they can convince people in your corner to turn their backs on you, and they can definitely hurt your feelings.

I know that being able to separate from people whom you've known for years, who are now mistreating you or undermining your growth, is not easy. To get through it, I believe that you have to be strong in the Word. You have to spend time with God. You need to get in a church that's teaching and not just singing. Get in that Bible study on Wednesday, because those lessons, and that spiritual guidance, are the tools that can keep you strong and give you comfort.

You also have to surround yourself with smart and positive people who are going places. Once you do, you'll look back and think, "Why was I hanging around with that other guy all of that time?" If you listen to inspirational figures like Steve Harvey or Oprah Winfrey and start hanging around with individuals who breathe life into you, you'll feel silly for doing what you were doing for as long as you were doing it. You'll think, "All of this time, I could have been over here. I could have been doing this. I could have been creating that. I could have been achieving and discovering so much more than I'd ever imagined before."

When you're trying to soar, you have to make sure that anybody you invite along for the ride is there to lift you up, not weigh you down. Once I realized how many good things came my way when I stood strong in faith and let go of people who were trying to hurt me, I no longer cared what anybody who wasn't helping to pay my bills thought about me. I focused on those who were feeding me good energy, the people who came to see me perform and supported my growth as a comedian. Steve Harvey has never said anything bad about me, and he has given me some of the biggest breaks in my career. I care about what *he* thinks, not someone who's never offered me a positive word. My manager, who represents some of the biggest legends in Hollywood, has always treated me well. So I'm not worrying about somebody who doesn't want to hang out with me after I tried to give them an opportunity and it didn't work out. I don't need them.

And I've also learned another truth. Sometimes, if you have to make a tough decision and distance yourself so you can succeed, a true friend will completely understand why you needed to take that step.

A couple of years ago, I had an old buddy, Willie Hudgins, whom I hired to be my driver and music director. But he wasn't doing the paperwork that he was required to do, and I had to let him go. It was an especially tough time to do it, because Thanksgiving was coming up. But I had a lot of people on my payroll, working on my shows, counting on me, and I couldn't jeopardize their livelihoods in order to spare my friend's feelings.

Thanksgiving morning arrived. I love to cook, so that's a big day for me. The candied yams were bubbling, the collard greens were simmering, and the turkey was just about ready to come out of the oven. My kids and I were pulling the plates out of the cabinets so that we could set the table. We were getting ready to turn on the television and watch some football when my doorbell rang. I opened the door, and do you know who was standing there? Willie Hudgins.

"What's up?" I asked.

"What do you mean 'What's up?'" he asked. "I came to eat."

I can't lie. For a second, I looked at him like he was crazy.

"You came to eat?"

"Yeah," he said, looking at me like *I* was the fool. "I don't care about getting fired. We're friends."

That meant everything to me. I had so much respect for him in that moment. To come to my house the day after we parted ways at work and have Thanksgiving dinner with my family and me took guts and a lot of class. That's how it's supposed to be. It also meant that he understood the true meaning of friendship, that just because someone close to you tells you that you're wrong, or has to take an action that might hurt a bit, it doesn't mean the whole relationship has to disappear. Willie and I are close to this day.

It's hard to walk away from people you've known or loved a long time. If you don't have a whole lot of people in your corner to begin with, it's even harder. But if you're sticking with folks who are holding you back or, worse, putting you down, the harsh truth is that you are already alone. There are other people out there who want to give you guidance, support, and friendship. You don't need a million people to have your back. One strong role model and a few supportive friends can make up for a whole bunch of folks you may have to leave behind. I don't care if you're poor and living in a housing project or if you don't have a mother or father to lean on; you can make something of yourself. You can be great at whatever you choose to pursue. But you've got to be around some eagles.

I'm excited about my life. I'm excited about *your* life, so get out of your own way. Step out of your comfort zone. Grow. Go somewhere. Instead of heading to the club, buy a ticket for a charity's fund-raiser. Put on a suit or a beautiful cocktail dress, get your hair cut, then print up some business cards and prepare to network. It may be a little uncomfortable. It may be a little scary. But you are bound to grow. It's hard to explain, but success and self-confidence just start to rub off on you.

If you fell into a garbage can and took your time getting out of it, the stench would follow you wherever you traveled. People at the gym, shoppers at the mall, and your coworkers at the office would smell you coming from a mile away. Associating with negative acquaintances can have the same effect. Their toxic nature lingers, crushing your spirit and repelling the positive people who might otherwise enter your orbit.

But when you stand near a perfume counter, all that sweet fragrance wafting in the air starts to cling to you. And you'll end up smelling like a rose.

You aren't like anybody else. Nobody has your fingerprints or DNA. You are unique. You are not a chicken. You are an eagle. So break out of that flock and fly, because as soon as you do, God has got some blessings waiting on you.

ON FORGIVENESS

I never question the presence of God, but sometimes I wonder about the ways some people use His name.

I think about how slave masters used religion as a way to oppress the people they'd enslaved, how they got them to holler about Jesus so that they'd be distracted from their pain.

I've watched the actions of one of my former pastors who I believed was misusing the church's money. All the goodwill that he preached flew straight out of the window when I dared to challenge him, and he chastised and criticized me right from the pulpit.

But I've never questioned the reality of a living God. I know that neither the president nor the pope made the sun come up. I know there's a power in the universe so strong that the leaves turn brown right on time and fall to the ground so that fresh green buds can take their place.

I know that there is a living God, because I can feel him. And just like I know there is infinite good, I also realize that there is evil. I want to walk on the side of good because one day I want to see God's face, and that means learning to forgive and leaving justice up to the Lord.

"Do not fret because of those who are evil or be envious of those who do wrong," says Psalm 37; "for like the grass they will soon wither, like green plants they will soon die away. Trust in the Lord and do good; dwell in the land and enjoy safe pasture."

Men may have written the Bible, but I believe Psalm 37 is definitely a message from on high. That scripture lets you know that there are evildoers and that they may hurt you, but God will come through and make it all right in the end. I held tight to those words in the days, weeks, months, and even years after a man tried to kill me.

———————

I JUST HAPPENED to be in the wrong place at the wrong time.

It was June 16, 1994. I was driving through my old neighborhood when I spotted my childhood buddy Johnny Spragg. Those were the days before everyone had an iPhone or Samsung Galaxy in their pockets, so Johnny was standing at a phone booth, about to put his dime in the slot to make a call. He put the receiver down when he saw me and gave me a big smile.

I pulled over and parked so that I could say a quick hello. When I stepped to the booth, out of the corner of my eye, I noticed three guys walking quickly toward us. I'd barely gotten the words "Hey, Johnny," out of my mouth when one of the men pulled a gun out from under his jacket and pointed it at Johnny's chest.

"Give it up, dude," he barked.

"I don't have nothing," Johnny said, his eyes darting from the guy with the gun to the other two men who were standing behind him. Then, suddenly, the gunman whipped around. His movement had to have been lightning quick, though in my memory it creeps along like a never-ending bad dream.

At point-blank range, he aimed a twelve-gauge shotgun at me and pulled the trigger. He must have fired more than once, because I was hit in my left side and in my elbow. I took off running, my insides burning from the buckshot as I darted between cars driving along Airport Highway.

I was literally running for my life. The twenty-third psalm raced through my mind, matching the rhythm of my pounding heart.

"The Lord is my shepherd. I shall not want."

I was panting and bleeding, but with my last breath, I was determined to say every one of the twenty-third psalm's words.

"He maketh me to lie down in green pastures. He leadeth me beside the still waters."

I ran up to a house and started pounding on the front door, begging anyone inside to please help me. The door didn't open.

"Yea, though I walk through the valley of the shadow of death I will fear no evil, for thou art with me. Thy rod and thy staff, they comfort me."

Blood was leaking from my wounds. I felt my life slipping away from me. "If I die," I prayed, "please, God, forgive my sins and welcome me into your arms."

I don't know how long I ran, but finally I couldn't do it anymore. I collapsed under a streetlight in the middle of a residential block.

Then, as quickly as the twenty-third psalm had sprung to my lips after I was first hit by that buckshot, my thoughts suddenly turned from dying to living. I thought about how if I died, it would kill my grandmothers, Ada and Mattie. I thought about how the only thing I wanted to do once more in this world was to talk to my mother, Carolita. I remembered how my grandparents had to bury my father, Ernest Jr., when I was a little boy and how much it hurt me to see their pain.

I had to get to my mother. I had to see my grandparents. I had to survive for my family. I stopped getting ready to die. And God stepped in.

There were two guys sitting on a porch nearby, drinking beer. One of them I knew slightly and the other man happened to be a nurse. He ran to me, tore off my shirt, and began to apply pressure to my wounds while the guy I was acquainted with ran into the house and dialed 911.

The next thing I knew, I heard police sirens and the blare of an ambulance. A police officer shone a light in my eyes and began to ask a lot of questions. I told him that when I'd started running, I heard two more gunshots. I figured they'd fired at Johnny and he was probably dead. He'd had a motorcycle accident not long ago and injured his leg, so I doubted that he was able to run away.

I was twenty-five years old. I'd performed on *Def Comedy Jam* and BET's *Comic View*. I was earning good money telling jokes at some of the hottest comedy clubs in the South. I had been welcomed into a fraternity of talented comedians—Steve Harvey, Mo'Nique, Cedric the Entertainer. I'd also gotten married for the first and only time in my life, to a beautiful flight attendant named Terri. I had so much to live for, but I wasn't sure that I was going to make it.

Lying in the ambulance, I thought that the paramedic who stuck the IV in my arm looked familiar. He was an older guy. Maybe I'd seen him in the audience at one of my shows, or maybe he grew up in the Kingston Projects like me. Maybe he had a relative who lived in my grandparents' neighborhood, or had once visited my church. Anyway, in that moment I desperately needed someone, anyone, to talk to. And it was good to see a familiar face.

"Hey, man," I whispered. "Am I going to live or die?"

I'll never forget what happened next. He leaned down toward me, and he said my name. "Don't worry, Rickey," he said. "I've seen worse. You're going to be all right. You're good. You're good." Then he grabbed my hand and held it in a tight grip all the way to Carraway Methodist Medical Center.

I wish I knew that paramedic's name. I would do anything to find him today, just to say thank you.

Birmingham can be a small town, and I've always made an effort to be kind to people. Now, during one of the scariest times of my life, it felt like all of those connections I'd made kept showing up to comfort me. I was acquainted with one of the men on the porch who saw me collapse and then called 911. The paramedic who treated me in the ambulance somehow knew my name. And when members of the hospital staff put me on a gurney and wheeled me down the hallway, I saw someone else that I recognized, though I again wasn't exactly sure where I knew him from.

"You're straight, Rickey," he said reassuringly. "We're going to put you to sleep for a little while and get you ready for surgery."

Right before I was given anesthesia to knock me out, one of the doctors who would be performing the operation came to talk to me. Before he could ask me a question or tell me what would be happening, I began speaking, my words tumbling out in a rush. "My name is Rickey Smiley. I work at the Comedy Club. Bruce Ayers is my boss. You can call him at . . ."

I was trying to live, and I wasn't sure that every doctor treated every patient with the same care. I wanted the doctor to know that I was a hardworking person whom people depended on. *Please don't dismiss me*, I was trying to say. *Please save my life.*

I also gave the hospital staff my grandmothers' names and their phone numbers. I can't imagine what it was like for someone to call them at three in the morning, telling them that their grandson had been shot. Even now, I don't want to think about how they must have felt in that terrible moment.

Several hours later, I woke up from surgery. My mother and stepfather were there. Mom had on a baseball cap and some shades. My grandfather Ernest was there, too, hovering over me. There were tears streaming down his face. It was only the second time in my life I'd seen him cry. The first time had been at his son's—my father's—funeral.

Forgiveness is hard. I know. I've been there. A stranger had fired buckshot into my body. My grandfather had to look at me lying in a hospital bed. Someone had woken my mother up from a deep sleep and told her that her only son had been shot. How could I forgive the man who put me and the people I loved most in the world through all of that?

It's easy to hold on to a grudge, to let resentment wrap around you like a protective blanket. You can use an old betrayal as an excuse to get out of doing the things that you are supposed to do, or as the reason you didn't achieve the goals you'd been talking about since you were eleven years old.

Chasing revenge is the easier path. But I also know that there is no justice like God's justice, just like there is no love like God's love.

THE DAY THAT I was baptized, I felt like I'd gone straight to heaven.

Church always made me feel good. The choir would sing "God Specializes," my grandmother Ada's favorite song, or "I Can't Pay the Lord," and I would feel full and happy. It was like joy was radiating from all the church members—the sisters in their over-the-top hats and the deacons in their pressed suits—and shining right on me.

Even when I was just eight years old, sitting next to my grandmothers, Ada and Mattie, I knew to be thankful—thankful that I'd never missed a meal; thankful that I'd never slept outside; thankful for Saturday evenings, when my older relatives and their friends drank

Jack Daniel's mixed with Coke and cracked jokes all night long, and I sat there listening and laughing until the tears flowed from my eyes.

My baptism was on a Wednesday evening. Our family attended New Mt. Olive, but since it didn't have a baptismal pool, we went to Groveland Baptist Church for the actual service.

First they baptized Lisa Wells, because she was the only girl in the group. Then they baptized Tony Jones. I was next. Then it was Lisa's brother Eric Wells's turn. The last one to go into the water was Derrick Barfield.

When my moment came, I remember looking out into the congregation and seeing my Sunday school teacher, Miss Hattie Freeman, with tears in her eyes. And I saw my grandmothers out there, too, sitting next to each other in the pew, their emotions bubbling up, on the verge of overflowing. My great-grandmothers Cherry Smiley and Delia Reed were also there.

I just felt special. It felt awesome.

I was baptized by Mr. Dow, one of the deacons at New Mt. Olive, and by our church's pastor, Reverend Edward Gardner. As each of us approached the pool, the congregation sang.

"Take me to the water."

The baptismal pool, set on a platform, towered above the congregation. As I walked down the steps, approaching the water, I glanced down at my grandmothers again. They wiped the tears from their cheeks.

"Take me to the water . . . To be baptized."

All of a sudden there were hands all around me, on my shoulders and on my arms and my back. I had butterflies in my stomach. What was this going to be like? I'd never been baptized before.

Reverend Gardner's voice rose like thunder. "In obedience, I baptize you now, my child. In the name of the father, and of the son, and of the Holy Spirit."

He put his hand over my face, leaned me back, and plunged me into the water.

Whoosh!

When I came back up, the singing started again.

"None but the righteous."

Miss Brown and Miss Wells, two of the older sisters at New Mt. Olive, were right there, standing at the edge of the pool with towels to wipe my face. As a matter of fact, Miss Wells is still there at my child-hood church. She must be in her seventies now, and she's still got a towel, wiping the faces of children right after they are officially wel-comed into the Lord's fold. Those old folks just made you feel special and protected. They magnified God's love.

That night, my mother bought me a couple scoops of vanilla ice cream at a popular local spot called Spinning Wheel to celebrate. I re-member looking out of the window of the car as the sweet cream dripped down the side of the cone.

Sunday couldn't come fast enough. My grandfather had told me after the baptism service that he was proud of me and that now I could take the Lord's Supper. That's what we call Communion in Alabama, and you couldn't receive it until you were baptized. On Sunday, finally, it would be my turn.

When the deacons brought the tray out with the Communion wa-fers, I started trembling. I was sitting in between my grandparents, wearing a new gray suit. I don't know if I was just excited to finally be tasting the Lord's Supper, but that first Communion cracker was as sat-isfying as that vanilla ice cream I'd had four days before at Spinning Wheel.

Then Reverend Gardner held up a goblet. "This," he bellowed, "is the blood of Jesus." As the deacons came around with the tiny paper cups of purple liquid, I was sitting there thinking, "Is this real blood? Is it wine?" All I knew was that I'd better not spill a drop of it on my white shirt. I took a sip and rolled the sweetness of Welch's grape juice around in my mouth.

Being baptized made me feel like I had graduated to another stage of life. I could receive Communion, just like all the grown folks. It also meant that I could join the youth usher board, which was run by a lady named Miss Beucray who lived across the street from the church.

The junior ushers wore white shirts and light blue ties as wide as bibs. We were responsible for passing out and collecting the envelopes that contained the congregation's tithes. We also had the very important job of fanning members of the church when they caught the Holy Ghost.

When members of the church caught the Holy Ghost, it meant that they were so joyful in the Lord and his goodness that they couldn't contain their emotions. They would leap out of their seats, jumping and shouting and flapping their hands in the air. And let me tell you, nobody got happy like Big Mama.

Big Mama's actual name was Helen, and she was married to my mother's father, Alan Bush. They lived in Cleveland, and every year I would travel there to spend at least part of the summer with them.

Big Mama was the first person I ever saw get happy. I was about five years old, and believe me when I tell you that she threw a serious, Holy Ghost–catching Baptist fit. That's when they get so happy that their shoes fly off and somebody has to pull them up from the floor and put their hat and glasses back on.

First, Big Mama started waving her arms and hitting me in the chest. I thought I had done something wrong and she was giving me a whack. But I soon realized Big Mama wasn't paying attention to me.

She didn't seem to even realize I was there. She started shouting. Then she dropped to the floor. I didn't know what the heck was going on. Was she having a seizure? Was she possessed? I was scared to death.

Somebody snatched me out of the way and hustled me over to another pew while members of the church tended to Big Mama. All those Cavaliers fans who think LeBron James is strong never saw Big Mama when the Holy Ghost took over. My mother says that it usually took three ushers to hold her down. That particular day, a church nurse had to run and get smelling salts to keep her from completely passing out. When Big Mama finally became calm, her hat was crooked, her wig was sitting sideways, and her skin was glistening with perspiration. But the Baptist fit had passed—for now.

You couldn't predict at exactly what point in the service Big Mama was going to catch the Ghost. Sometimes she'd be leading the choir, singing "Teach Us, Lord, How to Wait." Everything would be going fine. Her voice would be strong, and she and the other men and women in their lavender robes would be rocking in unison.

Then, all of a sudden, you'd notice Big Mama rocking left when everybody else would be rocking to the right.

"Uh-oh," I thought.

Then she'd start shaking her head. Then Big Mama would just stop singing and start shouting into the microphone. The ushers would rush onto the stage, and the choir members would just look at one another, panicking, not knowing how in the world they were going to finish the song. It would be absolute chaos.

It became a ritual. Sunday school? Check. Collection plate getting passed around? Check. Big Mama getting so happy her shoes flew off? Double check.

Big Mama would sometimes be so worn out after one of her Holy Ghost episodes that she would send me to get her purse and keys and we would just head home. That was enough excitement for one day.

I never really understood why Big Mama went into those convulsions. I think I was too scared to ask. But when I went back to Birmingham, I saw some of the other members of our church doing the same thing. I actually thought that they were just copying my grandmother in Cleveland. "They need to do their own thing and stop trying to be like Big Mama," I would think. I actually believed that Big Mama was the first person to have ever caught the Holy Spirit.

Finally, when I saw what must have been the tenth church sister jumping around and practically knocking people out, I asked my grandmother Mattie what was going on.

"Oh, she just got happy," Grandma Mattie said.

"She doesn't look happy to me," I said. My next thought I kept to myself: "If that's feeling happy, I'd rather feel sad."

As scary as it was to try to calm people who seemed to have lost their minds and who were also twice my size, I was proud to be on that usher board. It felt so formal and prestigious. The pastor would praise us every Sunday, saying how handsome we looked and asking the congregation to give us a round of applause.

We'd stand at attention like sentries, each of us with his big blue tie. We were shining like new dimes, a half jar of petroleum jelly slathered on our faces and so much grease in our hair that we looked like Mister, the character played by Danny Glover in *The Color Purple*, when he went to the juke joint to see Shug Avery.

We smelled good, too, usually like a pile of fresh laundry. That's because the night before, most of us had bathed in water so hot that we practically boiled to death. Forget Bed Bath & Beyond. There weren't any of those stores around. My grandmothers just tossed a cup of Tide detergent powder in the tub. You sat down and felt like you were at the beach, plopped on top of a mound of sand. Then, when bath time was over, you had to deal with an itchy backside that was white as chalk from the Tide.

What was the solution to that? More petroleum jelly.

WHEN I WOKE up after my surgery, the television was on in my room. I lay there, woozy, with tubes up my nose, and saw this white Bronco creeping along a freeway in Los Angeles with police cars on its tail. It was that famous chase, broadcast around the world, when O. J. Simpson was on the run. It turns out that I got shot four days after Nicole Simpson, O. J.'s ex-wife, and her friend Ron Goldman were killed in Brentwood.

I was in the hospital for three weeks. While I was there, I found out that Johnny had survived. He'd been wearing a cast, but I guess adrenaline overtook the pain that night at the phone booth. He cleared a fence like an Olympic hurdler and jumped into someone's backyard to get away.

Since I was in the intensive care unit, I could only have two visitors at a time. I had an oxygen mask on my face and tubes running in and out of me. When my friends came in the room, I knew that as bad as I looked, they weren't sure whether I was getting better or barely hanging on.

I felt like I needed to lighten the mood in that sterile place. So I started tightly closing my eyes when my buddies stopped by. Then, as they stood awkwardly next to my bed, I'd act like I was having trouble gathering the strength to move my hand.

I'd strain and struggle. You could feel the tension build in the room and practically hear a pin drop. Then, finally I'd manage to lift my hand a few inches above the bed and I'd shoot them the bird.

"Aw man," they'd yell out, laughing with relief. "You are an a--hole, Rickey!"

I did all of that to calm them down. I was getting stronger every day, but I knew that I didn't look like it. They were there to give me comfort and I wanted to give them a little back.

It wasn't just my old friends who came streaming through. So did the new friends I'd made in those early days of my career. Flex, the comedian who had a reality show on OWN and is married to the beautiful singer Shanice, is a good friend of mine. He stopped by the hospital to visit. I remember that Cedric the Entertainer called me on the phone and prayed with me.

I was really skinny even before I got hurt, and Steve Harvey made a joke during one of his shows that if I hadn't hidden behind a stop sign the night that I was shot I would have been dead. That cracked everybody up, including me, and I later used that same joke in my act.

Tina Graham, who booked all the up-and-coming comics and who, along with a promoter named Bob Sumner, represented me when I got my spot on *Def Comedy Jam*, told me that she was going to make sure that my career didn't miss a beat. Sure enough, within the next two years she got me on a show on HBO called *Snaps*. It costarred Tracy Morgan and Mo'Nique.

We'd stand in a boxing ring telling "yo mama" jokes, and our show debuted long before Nick Cannon's *Wild 'n Out*, which had a similar setup. That show also came out years before Tracy hit it big on *Saturday Night Live*, Mo'Nique won an Academy Award for the film *Precious*, and *The Rickey Smiley Morning Show* was even a thought in my mind. We were just young, hungry comics having a ball.

While I was recuperating, Flex and the comic Maceo came from

New York a couple of times to fill in for me at the Comedy Club. Nate Smith, Kevin Hart's travel manager, also came to see me. I know all of that support helped me to heal. But I still had a long road ahead. When I finally got out of the hospital, I had been bedridden so long that I could hardly walk.

––––––––––

THERE WAS A different energy pulsing out on the streets. When word got out that I had been shot, the search was on for the guy who did it. I had built up goodwill. Folks felt I was a nice dude who helped people in the community and represented Birmingham well. In short, I was good in the hood. Whether they were hustling in the streets or teaching in a Birmingham classroom, people were proud of Rickey Smiley.

Forget that no-snitching foolishness you hear about nowadays, where people think it's honorable to not tell on people who victimize their friends and neighbors. People who take advantage of and hurt others need to be on notice that they cannot hide. And Birmingham wasn't playing around with the guys who attacked me and Johnny. The man who shot me was named Jeremy Anderson, and the streets turned him in. He rode around town in a Caprice Classic with tinted windows, and he and his crew were known for going around robbing people.

Not that I approved of it, but a few times it almost became a case of an eye for an eye. Someone fired a shot into the family home of one of Jeremy's accomplices. Then, one night, one of my cousins came face-to-face with Jeremy on the street.

He and Jeremy knew each other. And by now, pretty much everyone knew that Jeremy was the one who'd shot me.

My cousin was a pretty tough dude himself, and when he bumped into Jeremy, he whipped out the pistol he always carried and pointed it at Jeremy's head. I heard from others who were there to witness it that my cousin had tears running down his face and his finger on the trigger. He was seconds away from shooting Jeremy, but someone standing nearby talked him out of it.

Jeremy's days were numbered anyway. Someone finally tipped off the police, and Jeremy and his accomplices were arrested.

The trial date was months away, and time ticked on. I got stronger physically. I went back to work at the Comedy Club. I was performing in my own shows and getting to church every Sunday.

But mentally, I was rattled. I didn't like being out after dark. I was always alert as to who was approaching me or standing nearby. I was fearful. And I was angry.

The day of the trial, I put on a suit and drove to the courthouse. I stepped on the elevator. And do you know who I saw standing there? It was the man who'd pulled the trigger and shot me, Jeremy Anderson.

I'd heard that he was out on bail. I think that was part of the reason I'd felt so nervous all of those months. But now, in that elevator, riding up to the sixth floor, all I felt was rage. I stood and faced him, anger gripping my heart. He wasn't man enough to even look me in the eye. He looked down at the floor, up at the elevator lights, anywhere but at me.

That was probably the longest elevator ride of my life, and when we hit the sixth floor, you'd better believe I let him get off first, because I damn sure wasn't going to let him walk behind me.

I took the stand during Jeremy's trial. That man's face had been etched in my mind since that night in June. I told the jurors that I would never forget it. And they believed me. He was found guilty and sentenced to twenty-five years in prison.

The desire for revenge can take your breath away. I know it. I've been there. Forgiveness is hard.

———————

JEREMY WENT TO jail, and my life took off. I won custody of my oldest son, Brandon, and became a full-time dad.

My career was also accelerating. I was selling out venues across the country. I began appearing on the radio for the first time, cracking jokes and making prank calls alongside the radio personalities Africa and Buck Wilde. I later landed a spot on the nationally syndicated Doug Banks radio show, and then left Birmingham for Dallas to host a radio show of my own. When my show made it to number one in its format, I got a syndication deal that led to my eventually being on the air in dozens of markets, from Orlando to St. Louis.

I met beautiful, dynamic women, and became a father and a force in the lives of a whole village of children who were and weren't biologically mine. My life was moving, sometimes at a speed faster than a kid growing up in the Kingston Projects could have ever imagined.

But getting shot scarred me physically and mentally. All the support from my family, the love of my fans, and the success of my career couldn't wipe away the memory of that night in June. That frantic run for my life, the pain in my side, the weeks it took for me to regain the strength to walk again on my own, stayed with me. I couldn't shake it.

To this day, it hurts to rest my left elbow on a table. Because of the potential nerve damage that it could have caused to remove them, I still have a couple pieces of buckshot lodged next to my bone, so I have to adjust my arm, basically shifting the buckshot around, to rest my elbow in comfort.

During that initial emergency surgery, the doctors had to repair my large and small intestines. At first they believed I would have to spend my life connected to a colostomy bag, but God was merciful and that wasn't necessary. Still, the injury to my arm affected the muscles in my left hand. My doctors said I would eventually develop arthritis. And when I go for my annual physical, some of the buckshot left in my side—because, like my elbow, removing it might have caused even more damage—shows up on the X-ray. I feel embarrassed having to explain why it's there.

I was angry. And I lived in fear for a long time. Anytime I saw a Caprice Classic with tinted windows roll by, I felt totally terrified, even though Jeremy Anderson was locked away in the Holman Correctional Facility in Atmore, Alabama. When I drove past one of those old cars, I would check that my doors were locked and try to speed away.

All these years later, if I don't have a comedy show to do, you can barely get me to leave my house after six o'clock. A key reason is plain old leftover fear from the day I encountered Jeremy.

You can't pay me to make a hard stop at a red light. I always slow down in the middle of the block and time the light so when I get to the corner it's green and I can put my foot on the gas.

My grandfather had taught me to do that when he was teaching me how to drive. But I applied his wisdom to more than driving after I got shot.

When I go to different cities to perform, I have rules for the road. If I get paid in cash, the promoter doesn't know who I'm riding with. I provide my own transportation, even if it's a fraternity brother who lives in town driving a random car. I will slide out of the theater's side door and disappear. I move safely and smoothly.

And I don't embrace the flashy celebrity lifestyle. I've never bought a set of gaudy rims for my car. I don't wear jewelry. When I walk through the airport, headed to a flight, I wear a Nike sweat suit, a Nike cap, and a backpack holding the outfit that I will wear onstage. I get sharp as hell at the arena before I do my show, but I'll slip right back into my sweat suit when my show is done, and then get out of Dodge. I am a magician when it comes to vanishing.

———————

I BELIEVE IT was in 2013 that Jeremy Anderson came up for parole. It had been nearly twenty years since that night at the phone booth in Birmingham. I headed to Montgomery for the parole hearing.

My heart was still hard. This fool, trying to cop a drug, or snatch some cash, ripped away my sense of security and clouded the way I viewed the world.

I sat in the small hearing room where the parole board was going to convene. I wanted Jeremy to serve every remaining minute of his time. He hadn't taken my life, but he had cast a shadow over it. He needed to pay.

And that's what I intended to tell the board. Until I looked over and saw Jeremy's mother.

She was a small lady wearing a simple dress, with a deep brown complexion and a little gray in her hair. She seemed to be a nice person. And I felt sorry for her. Here was a mother, hoping that her son would get out of prison, sitting before a panel that held his freedom in its hands.

He'd been locked up for nearly twenty years, and who knew how much more time his mother had to live? Just that fast, my heart started to turn, and I felt that this hearing, this situation, wasn't just about me anymore.

"Mr. Smiley, would you like to make a statement?" a member of the parole board suddenly asked.

I got to my feet and I started to tear up. It was hard to stand in front of that man's mother and say that her son needed to stay in prison. Thoughts started rushing through my mind.

He was just a kid when he committed his crime. He'd done wrong, but he'd been punished. After all these years, it was time for me to embrace the spirit of reconciliation. Let the man go on home to his mother, so all of us could get on with our lives. God knew that I'd had a great one. I didn't die that night. I'd gone on to achieve more success than I'd ever dreamed of. I had a beautiful family and wonderful friends. Let this woman have her son back.

"I think Mr. Anderson has paid for what he did . . ." I began, my voice shaking.

"Let me stop you right there, Mr. Smiley," the man on the parole board said, cutting me off as he picked up a file. He started flipping through it and then turned his attention to Jeremy's mother.

He read the details of a crime. "Ma'am," he said, "did you know your son did this while he was in prison?"

"No, sir," she said.

He read off another crime. "Did you know your son did that while in prison?"

"No, sir."

"Right now your son is in solitary confinement," he finally said. "We were obligated to hold this hearing, but I have to tell you that we don't parole anybody who is currently in isolation."

So in the end, it didn't matter what I had to say. Jeremy Anderson had to stay in prison.

———

I DIDN'T GO to Montgomery for any more hearings, but about five years later, I received a letter saying that Jeremy had been released. I figured that he would return home to Birmingham.

By that time, I had a docuseries, *Rickey Smiley for Real*, that was centered on me and my kids. A new storyline popped into my mind. I wanted to find Jeremy and have a conversation with him. I wanted to ask him if I could help him find a job. I wasn't going to hire him myself, but I knew some people who might. This wasn't about me. I wanted to help him get back on his feet so that he wouldn't return to committing robberies and make somebody else the victim of his bad decisions.

I wanted to feature it all on my show. I pictured scenes where I talked about and demonstrated forgiveness, telling a story about someone who had hurt me and whom I helped to get back on track. I wanted to show how we can help break the cycle of people coming out of prison and going right back to hurting people, and also demonstrate how forgiveness can help the victim as well as the victimizer.

I asked my producers to try to locate Jeremy, and they did. We were looking into setting up a meeting with him when I checked my Facebook feed one morning. I saw a bunch of posts asking me if I'd heard the news. Jeremy had been killed the night before. We were from the same general neighborhood, so we knew many people in common. Apparently, Jeremy was killed drag racing his sister's car.

Jeremy's body lay in the county morgue for days. Though I wasn't able to help Jeremy in life, when I heard that, I thought I might be able to give some assistance to Jeremy's mother, whom I'd seen five years earlier, as well as the rest of his family. But in the end, it wasn't necessary. I learned that Jeremy's uncle came through and was able to pay for his burial.

One of our mutual acquaintances mentioned what day the funeral would be, but I didn't intend to go. I figured that my connection with Jeremy was done.

A few days later, after I did my radio show from home, I hopped into my Jeep to run a couple of errands. It was a summer day, so I had taken the doors off and was blasting Fleetwood Mac, my favorite group. I was rolling down First Avenue toward my mother's house to take her some black-eyed peas I'd cooked the night before, when I drove past a funeral procession.

I couldn't make this up if I tried. It was Jeremy's.

I knew it was his as soon as I saw it. His relatives and friends were flowing out of the Eastside Funeral Home. I think just coming upon Jeremy's funeral scared me more than the night he'd shot me. It just felt creepy, like I would never be able to get away from this man, even in death. I got paranoid, feeling like somebody was going to jump out of one of the family cars in the procession, or even the hearse, and come after me in retaliation for Jeremy's spending so many years in prison.

Then I thought of Psalm 37 and I started to calm down: "Do not fret because of those who are evil or be envious of those who do wrong; for like the grass they will soon wither, like green plants they will soon die away. Trust in the Lord and do good; dwell in the land and enjoy safe pasture."

I had not been vengeful. I had worked hard to forgive. I was going to argue for Jeremy to be released from prison at his parole hearing. I was willing to help the man who tried to kill me find a job, and I was even going to give money toward his funeral expenses, if his family couldn't afford it.

Now Jeremy was dead, and I hadn't lifted a finger in retaliation. I'd tried to do the right thing by a man who had done a terrible thing to me. I had nothing to fear.

I do believe that often you die because it's your time. But I also believe that sometimes you hasten that moment with your own bad decisions. Jeremy finally had a second chance at life, and he squandered it drag racing in his sister's car, putting others in danger as well as himself.

In the end, whether it was his destined time to go or he sped up the clock, he was gone. I'd never run into him again, driving by in a Caprice or walking up behind me on a street corner. I didn't have to worry that my plans to try to help him would backfire and he would hurt me or someone else.

Forgiveness is hard. I don't think I even began to search for it in my heart until twenty years after I was shot and I faced the mother of the man who committed the crime. Over the next five years, I still had days when I strained not to feel angry.

There are situations in all of our lives that test us. You're betrayed by a friend, mistreated by a boss, abused by a stranger, and it can be hard to imagine ever pardoning what they did.

But revenge can be tougher on you than the person who did you wrong. It can poison you. It can blind you to your potential and all the brightness in your future.

Forgiveness is hard. I know. I've been there. But I also know that there's a higher power whose love for you is strong and whose ability to dole out justice is greater than yours or anyone else's. Overcoming a desire for revenge may be one of the most difficult things you ever have to do. It's like you have to get through an obstacle course of emotions, only you're not so sure it's a contest that you want to win.

But when you come to the end of the road—when you understand that each of us has faults, that all of us make terrible mistakes sometimes, and that love will defeat hatred every time, when you come out on the other side—you can find peace.

YOU'VE GOT TO DANCE WITH THE ONE WHO BROUGHT YOU

Think of all the people in your life who've done a favor for you. Maybe you were a little kid, really craving an ice-cream cone, but it turned out that you were a dime or a quarter short, and the ice-cream vendor gave you the cone anyway. Or you had a friend who saw you suffering because you really, really wanted that treat, and he was the one who coughed up the change that you needed to make it happen.

How about the girl who lived down the street and protected you when the neighborhood bully was hassling you, because you were the smallest kid on the block?

Or maybe you really needed a summer job in high school to help buy your outfits for the upcoming school year. You kept getting rejection after rejection from potential bosses. Then, just when you were about to give up and you'd resigned yourself to wearing those too-tight jeans from the year before, your English teacher told you about her cousin, whose accounting office was looking for an intern. She gave her relative your name, and you got the job.

In all those situations, the first thing to do is to simply say thank you. But later, you can do a lot more than that. Maybe your path and the one followed by the person who helped you out will go in different directions, and you'll never meet again. But if you ever have the chance to return that favor, however small it might have been, do it.

If you're a teenager and you spot the ice-cream vendor at the supermarket struggling to carry his groceries, help him tote the bags. If you run across that teacher years later, and she's older and frail, offer to take her to the doctor, if she needs a ride.

Say a kind word to the neighbor who once lifted your spirits when you were feeling low. Or if that friend who once stood up for you in a fight needs a couple of bucks, do what you can to help. You've got to dance with the ones who brought you to the party.

Too often, we are loyal to people who don't deserve it. We loan money to our best friend from kindergarten, even though he never pays us back. Whenever you need something—a babysitter to watch your kids for a few hours, a ride when your car is at the mechanic's garage—that same old friend can never be found.

If someone is badmouthing a person who was always nice to you, who gave you advice about how to file your taxes or steered you right when you were about to make a wrong turn, don't get involved in that conversation. And consider going the extra mile to let the trash-talker know what the person they're putting down once did for you.

I truly believe that when you do good deeds for others, God will triple your blessings, sending you a strong message that you made the right moves. And I also believe that ingratitude is a terrible thing. When you turn your back on those who've treated you well, or who just reminded you of your value when someone else was trying to make you forget it, you might discover that the next time you need a favor, there's no one there to help.

———————

WHEN I STARTED performing regularly at the Comedy Club in 1990, I was making only $100 an appearance, but I couldn't believe how lucky I was to get paid to tell jokes at all. The best part of the job was opening up for some of the funniest comics in the business. It was like I got to take a master class each of those Saturday nights.

The first big name I got to introduce was George Wallace. Being a tall, broad-shouldered African-American man with the same name as Alabama's segregationist onetime governor, George cracked up the crowd pretty much as soon as he walked out onstage. He was also one of the nicest guys you'd ever want to meet, and I really appreciated being able to warm up the crowd for him and then sit back and watch him go to work.

The second headliner I got to call to the stage was Rita Rudner. She was a former Broadway dancer who, when she decided to become a comedian, actually sat down and studied the jokes of classic comics like Jack Benny. She picked apart how he tackled humor the way an architecture student might analyze Frank Lloyd Wright's blueprints. She went on to host her own specials on HBO, and she's had a long-running one-woman comedy show in Las Vegas. If you had popped me in the backside with a red-hot poker, I couldn't have been any more shocked than I was when Bruce Ayers, the club's owner, told me that I would be opening up for her. Rita Rudner? I couldn't believe the people I was getting to work with.

I didn't pay a lot of attention ahead of time to who the club's headliners would be, because it didn't really make a difference to my routine. My job was always the same: crack jokes for about five minutes, and then get out of the way, so that the comedians the audience had paid to see could come out and take the stage.

But I knew when Steve Harvey was coming to town. He'd made an impression on me from the first time I met him.

It was back when I was still doing open mic night, before I got my upgraded gig. I got to the club, and Bruce asked me to come backstage. He wanted to introduce me to someone. That person would wind up becoming one of my closest friends, as well as probably my most important role model for how to navigate the worlds of business and entertainment.

"Come here, Rickey," Bruce said. "Meet Steve Harvey."

Steve was on a double bill with the comedian Carrot Top. He must have been about twenty-nine years old then, a decade older than me. He was tall, serious, and decked out in a pin-striped suit. He looked like he meant business.

"Steve," Bruce said as Steve and I shook hands, "this is Rickey. I think he's pretty funny. I want you to take a look at him and see what you think. Maybe you can help him out."

Steve would come back to the club often. And eventually, after Bruce had hired me as a host, I got the chance to introduce him. I'll never forget the first time. I was wearing a Nike sweat suit, my go-to outfit when I wanted to look cool and feel comfortable. Bruce never minded when I showed up casual. And it was a *nice* jogging suit. But Steve wasn't having it. He looked me up and down and then proceeded to school me about how I needed to present myself.

"Hey, dude," Steve said. "You're opening up for Steve Harvey, and I don't show up for work in a sweat suit. People are paying money to see us. I'll go ahead and let you introduce me tonight, but tomorrow, you need to dress better."

I'd been studying Steve, the way he could take command of the audience with just an expressive look on his face. This was many years before he had a hit movie based on his book *Act Like a Lady, Think Like a Man*, and before he hosted the *Steve Harvey* television series and *Family Feud*. But his talent was undeniable. He knew how to tap into the rhythm of the crowd. For forty-five minutes, the men and women huddled together at those tables could tune out the problems they had at the office, the tuition bills dangling over their heads, the medical report with bad news, and just laugh until their stomachs ached. And Steve made all that happen dressed so sharp that it looked like he was about to apply for a bank loan.

I took in his reprimand, then I walked out onstage, did a short routine, and announced him.

"Ladies and gentlemen, give it up for Steve Harvey!" I yelled.

We switched places under the spotlight, and I headed straight to my car and drove to my house. I dug through my closet for a suit I'd bought to wear to church, put it on, grabbed a tie, and then rushed back to the club.

By the time he was saying, "Thank you! Good night!" and exiting the stage, I was there, suited up and ready to rush out to tell the audience to keep the applause going.

After I wished the crowd a good evening and everyone started filing out, I found Steve standing to the side of the club, waiting for me.

"Okay," he said, checking out my suit, which wasn't as nice as his but I guess was good enough. "I'm going to help you, because I can see you're serious."

From then on, Steve took me under his wing. He introduced me to this comedian from St. Louis named Cedric the Entertainer and a hilarious, trash-talking young lady named Mo'Nique. I was getting to meet, learn from, and become great friends with the funniest young comics on the circuit.

In 1993, Steve started hosting *Showtime at the Apollo*, a gig that lasted five years. It was a variety show that featured the biggest acts in music, as well as up-and-coming comedians like me. It was held at the legendary Apollo Theater, where entertainers like Sarah Vaughan, Gladys Knight, and the Jackson Five had performed.

Whether or not the audience had those greats on their minds while they sat in those seats, they seemed to understand that if you dared to walk on that same stage, you had giant shoes to fill. I'd appeared there a few years before, when Mark Curry was one of the guest hosts, and they practically booed me back to Birmingham. But Steve was able to control the crowd. If he liked you, they liked you, and he introduced me like he was bringing up one of Jesus's best friends.

Then, a few years later, Steve gave me an opportunity that, to this day, makes me emotional when I think about it. He had me open up for the Kings of Comedy tour.

The Kings of Comedy first hit the stage in 1999. Steve, Cedric, D. L. Hughley, and the late, great Bernie Mac were packing auditoriums across the country, dishing and dissing about relationships, race, and the routine things that everybody experiences in life. The tour became such a phenomenon that Spike Lee directed a movie about it, filming the concert over two nights in Charlotte, North Carolina. The film debuted in 2000 and made the tour an even bigger hit. It also gave some much-deserved attention to a group of black comedians who had yet to cross over into the mainstream.

By the time the Kings came to Birmingham, my career was seriously taking off. I had done a steady stream of stand-up appearances around the country, and I was also featured on 95.7, a Tuscaloosa-based station whose signal reached Birmingham, with the comedic personalities Chris Coleman and Tammi Mac.

Tammi is the woman in that LifeLock commercial where the guy looking in a patient's mouth isn't really a dentist. Tammi confirms that the patient's teeth are in bad shape, then asks the fake dentist if he's ready for lunch. She's always had a great deadpan look and perfect timing. Steve was stopping by to talk to Tammi, Chris, and me to promote the Kings of Comedy concert that was happening that evening at the Birmingham-Jefferson Civic Center.

At the time, Steve was starring in *The Steve Harvey Show* on the CW network and since we'd first met about a decade earlier, he'd become one of the most popular African-American comedians in the country. He owned Birmingham. Even when he was the solo headliner, tickets would sell out in a few hours, and anybody lucky enough to snag a ticket buzzed about it for weeks before the show.

Now that he was back in town, there was a different kind of buzz ricocheting through the circles of comedians and radio personalities. Word on the street was that Steve had "changed." Some not-as-famous comics were saying that Steve thought that he was better than other folks now that he had become a big celebrity. They were saying that he "had an attitude."

I hadn't talked to Steve in a while, and so I didn't really know what to expect. I mean, my career had picked up steam, but I was cohosting a little old radio show on the air in Tuscaloosa and Birmingham, while he was filling theaters across the country and starring in his own television sitcom. Was he too big-time now to bother with me?

The morning of the interview, Steve rolled up to the station. He had always been no-nonsense, and when he wasn't performing, he was a man of few words. It's like he was conserving every ounce of energy for the time that he had to start cracking jokes for the audience. And sure enough, when that red light came on signaling that we were on the air, Steve came alive. He was sharp, charming, and funny as hell.

The four of us were going back and forth for a couple of minutes, swapping jokes, when Steve suddenly said he had an announcement. I thought maybe they were adding an extra night to the show, or he was going to make an unexpected appearance at a local mall to meet up with fans.

I was way off.

"You know what, y'all? Rickey Smiley is going to be opening the show tonight for the Kings of Comedy."

I was stunned. "For real?" I said. I was going to be part of the show with Bernie, D. L., Cedric, and Steve?

"Yep," he said, looking me dead in the eye.

As soon as I got off the air, I went into overdrive. I jumped in my 1995 Jeep Cherokee, and I must have driven ninety miles per hour to Atlanta to pick up my son Brandon. Under the custody agreement that I had with Brandon's mother, it was my weekend to have him, and I didn't care what was going on in my life, I *never* missed a weekend with my son.

Brandon hopped into my car and I whipped right around and drove back to Birmingham. Now I needed a new suit. Opening for the Kings of Comedy was going to bring a whole other level of attention. My $29 pants from Zara and my going-to-church suits from Jeans West (*Buy a jacket and pair of pants, get the shirt free!*) weren't going to cut it. So Steve, in addition to surprising me with an invitation to introduce him at that night's show, had also given me a couple hundred dollars to buy a new suit.

I stopped at a store, but it was hard to get a suit right off the rack that hung properly on my skinny frame. So next I needed to find a tailor. I knew a guy who I'd heard did good work and ran in his shop's front door.

Not only did the tailor hem and take in my suit, he also let me wash up in his bathroom in the back, because the clock was ticking down, and I didn't really have time to go back home. I grabbed paper towels and soap out of the dispenser, cleaned myself up, and put the suit on right there. Brandon sat in a chair outside, leafing through some comic books.

Brandon and I headed to the Civic Center. Steve had told me that I could share his dressing room. I knew that I was a guest, so when I got there, I curled into a corner with my new suit and my son, and I made sure that we both stayed out of the way. Steve was quiet, off to himself. I didn't take it personally. I already knew Steve's personality, and I respected who he was.

I sat there for a little while, still hardly believing that I was opening for the Kings of Comedy. Then the stage manager poked his head in and said, "All right, it's about that time." Steve got up, and he came over to talk to me.

"Hey. I want you to go onstage, do five minutes, and then introduce me."

"Got it," I said.

I rose from my chair and headed out. It might be hard to believe, but I wasn't nervous, just excited. By then, I was used to getting in front of a crowd and priming their funny bones. I knew that I was hilarious. And I knew that Steve knew that I was hilarious, because if he didn't think so, friend or no friend, there was no way he would have let me anywhere near that stage.

Plus, you can't get into a real routine in five minutes, anyway. I was going to go out there, tell a couple of jokes, and shout out all the neighborhoods around Birmingham, and then I'd be done. My focus was to make sure I introduced Steve the right way and that I did a good job getting the audience ready for him. And then I would be out.

So I went onstage and did what I was told and what I had planned. "All right, Birmingham! Are you ready for the Kings? Give it up for Steve Harvey!"

Now, I had gotten some laughs. I could feel the energy rippling through the auditorium. But when I introduced Steve? It was like the sergeant at arms had entered the halls of Congress and introduced the president of the United States. Steve hadn't been to the Comedy Club in a while, and Birmingham was eager to see him.

As Steve glided out, the music started blasting, lights started flashing, and plumes of smoke filled the air. Steve got a standing ovation and he hadn't said a word. I shook his hand and headed offstage.

I stopped for a second and turned around to take it all in. "Wow," I thought. "That's amazing."

I had turned back to the short staircase that led backstage when I heard Steve suddenly yell, "Hey! Stop the music! Everybody, stop, stop, stop."

I was startled. What was wrong?

"Hey, Rickey," he said. "Come back up those steps."

I walked back. I couldn't figure out what the heck was going on.

Steve put his hand on my back, and he spoke to Birmingham. "I'm gonna let you all know, this one here is the next one," he said. "This is your own. Rickey Smiley."

The applause from the crowd sounded like thunder. Everything—the bright white lights hanging from the ceiling, the crowd spread out in the room in front of me, Steve standing right there by my side—became a blur.

When someone with the level of stardom and respect that Steve had introduces you like that in front of your peers, your classmates, your family, there are no words for what that means. Suddenly, I was no longer Rickey from around the way, who was cool and funny but probably only going to make it so far. I was "the next one," sharing a stage with Cedric the Entertainer, D. L. Hughley, Bernie Mac, and Steve Harvey. Steve anointed me that night.

When I walked offstage, I didn't go straight to Brandon. I went to a bathroom, sat down on the toilet, and cried. I couldn't believe what Steve had done.

After that show, my hometown momentum became supercharged. To this day, if I perform in Birmingham at a comedy club that seats four hundred people, I'll fill that place every night, from one Monday to the next. I'll do three shows on Friday, three shows on Saturday, and three more on Sunday. People will stand in line to see their local boy. Steve Harvey had put me on the map.

That night at the Civic Center wasn't the end. It was the beginning. Steve called me not long after that show and told me he had talked to Walter Latham, the promoter who produced the Kings tour, and gotten him to agree to have me join the group for a few dates. I was going to continue to introduce Steve, and make $1,000 a night.

"We'll get your hotel room," he said. "But you'll have to pay for your own travel." I told him that I didn't have a problem with that.

Since I wasn't officially a "king," Steve also continued to let me share his dressing room. And I'd have to be in the hotel lobby by a certain time to ride with him to the venue in his limousine, because as the opening act, I also didn't get my own car. Back then there was no Uber.

Steve didn't have to do any of this. He didn't have to convince Walter Latham to let me continue to introduce him. Steve didn't have to share his space with me. He could have made me change in the bathroom, and catch cabs or rent a car. So I knew not to wear out my welcome.

Steve was generous with his space, but he wasn't trying to do a lot of chitchatting before the show. I stayed quiet and only spoke when I was spoken to. I respected his need for silence.

And that isn't just Steve's personality before a concert. In general, Steve is moody as hell. Even now, I know just how to mess with him. I'll call and say, "Hey! I heard the ratings on *Family Feud* are falling fast." After cursing me out for a second, he hangs up on me, and I crack up.

But all kidding aside, riding in that limousine with Steve, sitting in his dressing room, walking in his footsteps in order to introduce him, just made me feel thankful. I used to thank Steve so much that he started telling me to stop.

Once when I was leaving a rehearsal for *Def Comedy Jam*, I saw Steve across the street getting ready to head in. I started waving at him like a little kid happy to see his daddy coming home. Steve didn't even acknowledge me. He just shook his head and gave me that trademark look that seemed to say, "This dude is so country. I'm about sick of him."

But I didn't stop thanking him, and I never will. With maybe the exception of your parents, nobody has to do anything for you, and when they do, you need to thank them forever.

I never let my listeners claim that I'm bigger than the one who gave me some of my biggest breaks. I cut off fans who try to sneak in a dig like, "Your show is so much funnier than Steve's." I don't let other comics or radio personalities get in my head and make me think that I'm better than the man who helped set me up. I dance with the one who brought me to the party.

———

WITHOUT STEVE HARVEY, there probably wouldn't be a *Rickey Smiley Morning Show*. I was already doing really well. I had appeared on *Showtime at the Apollo*; I had hosted *Comic View* in 2000, and I would again in 2004, bringing my exposure to a whole new level. I'd appeared in *Friday After Next* with Ice Cube, Mike Epps, and Terry Crews, playing a character called Santa Claus.

My reputation and celebrity had grown to the point that I was making great money doing shows on the road. I had a beautiful home in an exclusive suburb of Birmingham with a pool and lake in the back. But *The Rickey Smiley Morning Show* enabled me to reach millions of people all over this country every day, to mix in messages about social justice, compassion, and God with my jokes and hip-hop. And Steve played a key role in my being able to do that by recommending that I take his place on KBFB 97.9 in Dallas. The success of that show got me a syndication deal. And now I am in about eighty radio markets, from Texas to Mississippi.

So I knew what I had to do the day that I got a call from the manager of a top hip-hop station in Orlando. He said that he wanted to take *The Steve Harvey Morning Show* off the air and replace it with mine.

"*The Rickey Smiley Morning Show* is growing," he said. "We want you here."

I told him that I needed to call him back. I immediately jumped in my car and drove down Peachtree Avenue to the Atlanta Civic Center, where Steve happened to be taping *Family Feud*. I told him that we needed to talk.

We went into a room. "Listen," I said. "They're going to take your show off in Orlando. And they're going to put my show on. How would you like me to handle this? Because I'm riding with you. Do you want me to quit this job and come be on your morning show?" I asked him. "What do you need for me to do, because I'll give it all up if you say so."

I meant every word. And Steve actually started crying. That room was so quiet, you could have heard an ant crawling across the floor. I didn't know what had triggered Steve's tears. Was he that upset about the idea of being off the air in Orlando? Did he feel stabbed in the back by the guy who ran that radio station?

Finally, Steve pulled it together enough to speak. He told me that I was one of the most loyal people that he'd met in his life, and he said that he considered me his best friend. "You take that job in Orlando," he said. "And you give it your all. Because what God has for me is for me. And what God has for you is for you." And he hugged me tightly.

I am always going to choose Steve. His ex-wife Mary has made some terrible allegations against him, including saying that he was unfaithful to her.

Now, if I believed that Steve had done awful things, I would have definitely had a conversation with him. But what I wasn't going to do was go out in public and put down my frat brother, my mentor, and one of my best friends, a man who changed my whole life. It is important to be loyal, to have the back of those who've had yours. Sometimes, you have to fight for those who've helped you, and prop them up when they are embattled and may not have the strength to defend themselves.

When I heard that Mary had gone on another radio show where she continued to criticize Steve, I went on my radio show and took up for my friend. I didn't play music for twenty minutes, and I just talked about Steve and Mary.

She had a son with this man, and for years, she benefited from his success. Why appear on a radio show so you can dog him out? Ask for alimony, child support, joint custody, and whatever you think you deserve. But why try to destroy his image, his reputation, and his career?

After I did that, when I next talked to Steve, there were more tears. He thanked me, and now it was my turn to tell him that he didn't have to. He had taken a chance on me years before at the Comedy Club. If he did something I felt was wrong, I would let him know, but I was never going to let somebody else talk about him. I am forever loyal.

I got another chance to show my commitment to our friendship in January 2017, when Steve met with newly elected president Donald Trump. He even got photographed with him in the lobby of Trump Tower. Steve said he had gone there at the request of President Barack Obama, and that he and Trump had talked about Steve's mentoring efforts and the need for programs and housing to help inner cities.

He didn't regret sitting down with Trump and engaging in dialogue, but social media caught fire. There were memes flying around portraying Steve as a sellout and a traitor to the black community. And people started blowing my phone up. "Hey, Rick. Something is going on with your boy Steve. You need to talk to him."

I did call Steve and we had a conversation about Donald Trump and what Steve did. But again, I wasn't going to go on the radio to speak about it. Anything that I had to say to Steve was going to be in private, man to man, friend to friend.

It's not about whether he's a Democrat or a Republican, or whether he supports Trump or doesn't. I may not agree with everything Steve does and says, but my love for him is unconditional.

I don't talk to Steve every day. Steve can be cranky and get on my last nerve. He calls me when he feels like talking, and if I don't hear from him, I know I need to leave his grouchy self alone. I know he's on *Family Feud*, hosting beauty pageants, doing radio, mentoring kids. And I'm just as busy as he is, so when he does pick up the phone, we usually rush past the greetings and get down to business. As high as I've risen, and as much as he's already done for me, he is still looking out for my career, suggesting that I host a show when he can't and mentioning other potential deals. He's been a blessing in my life. And I'll tell anybody that, whether they ask me or not.

———————

YOU NEED TO be loyal not just to the people who directly bring you to the party, who do an obvious favor for you, like getting you a job, giving you a reference, or recommending you for a gig. There are also those people who prepare you for the party in the first place. They are the folks who teach you skills, who show you right from wrong, and who give you the knowledge you need to navigate life.

I met Miss Alene Avery when I was in the sixth grade. Back then, they didn't have medicine for attention deficit disorder. Or maybe they did, but my mother didn't think about trying to get me any, or even having me properly diagnosed. She just figured I was a rambunctious kid who couldn't sit still, which was absolutely true.

I wasn't bad, just silly. I loved to laugh. I'd make faces and talk a little smack, but at ten or eleven years old, I think I was a better audience than I was a comedian. You'd pop out a joke or mimic the principal, and I would laugh so hard I would tumble to the ground. It made me popular, particularly with the kids who were the best trash-talkers, but it also earned me a seat right up by the teacher's desk, from the time I was in first grade all the way through middle school.

Most of my teachers would get exasperated, telling me to quiet down, and when that didn't work, they'd send me to the principal's office and occasionally give me a swat on my behind. But none of that stopped me. When the bell rang to start the next school day, I'd take my seat and prepare to laugh, cut up, and have a whole bunch of fun all over again.

That is, until I met Miss Avery. That woman kicked my butt. In her class at Anna Stuart Dupuy Elementary School, I had no control over anything. In that room, Miss Avery was the boss, the queen, the sun. She was completely, totally, indisputably in charge.

There were two sixth-grade classes at my school. One room was filled with the kids whose parents were still together, and the other had kids who were pretty much all being raised by single parents. That's the one I was in. We were also the ones who had the low test scores and were deemed to be a little slower on the uptake when it came to academics, and a little more in a hurry to get to recess. As a matter of fact, we'd start playing right in the classroom.

I was used to being in the "slow" class year after year, always with the same crew. We even went to summer school together for "strengthening." Our group had shared and shaken up a lot of teachers.

But my buddy Roosevelt Powell and I, and all the other boys and girls in our class, had never met a teacher like Miss Avery.

She was brown skinned with a double chin, and she looked over the top of her glasses like she was one of the pastor's aides at church. She was a graduate of Alabama State University, and she drove this big white car with a burgundy top. We would make fun of it behind her back all the time.

Miss Avery had no filter. I'm talking about this grown woman, standing at the blackboard with a piece of chalk in one hand and a math textbook in the other, talking about your mama. Then she'd dare you to go home and tell your mother what she'd said. We had met our match.

I think the first time that Miss Avery talked about my mother, my mouth dropped open. None of us could stand her. We'd walk quietly out to the yard when the bell for recess clanged and mumble among ourselves, "A teacher is talking about our mothers? Who the heck is she?"

But not long into the school year, we started thinking Miss Avery was funny—I mean *really* funny. We even started saying things just to rile Miss Avery up and get her going.

"Miss Avery, Jomo said something about your dress," someone would yell out.

"I don't know why," she'd spit back. "It's the same one his mama wore to church last Sunday." I would howl with laugher until my cheeks hurt.

Miss Avery used to wear these shoes with thick wedge heels that had circles carved out of the middle. She was heavyset, and when she walked, those wooden heels would bend until they looked like they were about to break. The jokes would fly. Jomo Williams, a classmate who remains one of my good friends to this day, was the main instigator. He would say, "Miss Avery has got those yo-yos on again," and we would laugh our heads off.

I really think that I started getting a sense of comic timing right then. Between my grandparents, who were so funny that they could have charged money for folks to come listen to them bicker, and my classmates like Jomo, I was learning how to read a room and find the funny in any situation.

Miss Avery also stood out in other ways. If one of the kids was talking to her and their breath smelled bad, she'd tell them not to breathe in her face. Then she'd reach into her desk, pull out a spare toothbrush and tube of toothpaste, and tell the kid to go to the bathroom to brush their teeth.

And she kept a little brown bottle of Sta-Sof-Fro hair oil in her desk, too. There was one kid who I don't think ever combed his hair. It was so kinky in the so-called "kitchen," that part of your scalp near the nape of your neck, that you knew it was going to hurt like heck to comb it out.

But Miss Avery would spray that oil on his rocky Afro, hand him a comb, and tell him not to come back from the bathroom until that stuff was smooth. It would take a while, but he looked like a little Michael Jackson when he walked back in the door. And soon, he no longer needed Miss Avery's hair oil and comb. He came to school every day with his hair picked out to perfection.

Gestures like that showed how much Miss Avery cared about us. She would talk about your mama and then act like your mama, making sure that you groomed yourself. She was instilling in us a sense of pride, letting us know that even though we were young, even though we had one parent at home and were stuck in the class for the "slow" kids, we were as good as anybody else. And we needed to take pride in how we looked, what we learned, and who we were.

We kids could get away with cracking a joke from time to time, and Miss Avery would give as good as she got, but most of the time, we had to buckle down and focus on our schoolwork. Back then, teachers were still able to give you a whack if you acted up, and you'd better believe that Miss Avery took full advantage of that privilege.

So did the school's principal, Rosa P. Hanks. If you ended up in her office, she'd beat your butt.

I spent a lot of time there, standing in the corner underneath the plaque that celebrated Ms. Hanks's sorority, Delta Sigma Theta. Ms. Hanks would stand back and hit me on the behind about four times with a paddle. It wasn't a brutal beating. It wasn't even enough to make you cry. The look on Ms. Hanks's face and the fact she was getting ready to hit you scared you more than the licking itself.

It did sting, though, like the whacks I'd sometimes get from my football coaches. And I'd feel embarrassed enough that I didn't want to get another licking or see that office again for a while. So I'd behave, at least for a couple of months.

When you went to the principal's office, you also had to pass by Ms. Hanks's secretary, Miss Robinson, who'd evidently gotten a tutorial in trash-talking from my teacher. Miss Robinson always had little comments to say. It was embarrassing enough getting spanked and having to stand all day in the principal's office without being fussed at by her.

Miss Robinson would look you up and down, stare at your shoes and your hair, and then she'd get started. "I can't believe you're sitting in school acting like a fool with your James Brown perm."

Allow me to explain where the put-down "James Brown perm" came from. You see, I didn't need Miss Avery's hair oil or her comb. Not only was my hair always groomed, but I also didn't have an Afro. My hair was relaxed, lying limp on my head, just like the hair on funk master Bootsy Collins, and the guys in the Ohio Players. A lot of the guys in groups like Earth, Wind & Fire and the Commodores had giant naturals, like Lionel Richie, but some of them—and those groups in the 1970s had about fifty members each—had straight locks, like Snoop Dogg wears now decades later.

So to be cool and to look like our music idols, many of us kids had perms. Your mother would roll your hair up at night, and the next morning, you'd pluck the rollers out. Then you'd run your fingers through your curls and head to school looking like an extra in the movie *Super Fly*.

But damn, Miss Robinson—James Brown?

––––––––––––––––

I THINK THE day that we felt our bond with Miss Avery most was when we found out that her mother had died.

She'd come to class one day, and in a kind of offhand way mentioned that she had to rush home after school, because people were coming to set up a hospital bed at her house. Her mother, she said, was very ill. I don't think my classmates and I thought too much about it. But the next day, when we arrived at class, Miss Avery wasn't there. The substitute teacher standing in her place told us that Miss Avery's mother had passed away.

We didn't know what to do, where she lived, or where the funeral might be. Even if we had figured that out, I'm not sure we would have gone. But the whole class was quiet, consumed with sadness. I remember that Easter was just a few weeks away.

We were only eleven years old, so we didn't really have deep conversations. We didn't go out and take a blood oath about how our behavior was going to change. But I think that moment was a turning point for each of us. From then on, we got more serious about our schoolwork. Our teacher had lost her mother. We had to do something for her.

Miss Avery was off for about a week and a half, and when she came back, I recall how quiet and better behaved we were. Without discussing it, without anybody's telling us what to do, we had decided to make her job easier. Even in the sixth grade, we had enough sense to chill out. We could feel her hurt.

Right before Easter break, I caught Miss Avery sitting at her desk, looking out of the window, with tears welling in her eyes. Earlier that day she'd told us how her mother would get her and her brothers and sisters all dressed up and ready for church every Easter Sunday.

I figured that's what she was thinking about as she looked out of the window, and it touched me. I'd never seen Miss Avery cry. I never believed she *could* cry. She was so tough that she was basically the school's designated disciplinarian. When other teachers had unruly kids in their classrooms, they would send them to Miss Avery to have her set them straight. But there she was, crying.

At the end of the school year, all of the kids in our class passed our final exams.

Despite her sometimes harsh ways, I realized that Miss Avery had made learning fun. Her "yo mama" jokes captured our attention and made us laugh. She'd have us work out math problems on the board instead of on paper, because that allowed the whole class to be involved. She knew that we were the students who had the lowest standardized test scores, and she pulled out everything in her arsenal to help us lift ourselves up.

She loved us. I have no doubt about that. And we worked really hard for her, and for ourselves, to catch up with that other group of sixth graders. Looking back, that was one of my best school years ever, because of all the laughs that I had, because of all the lessons that I learned, because of Miss Avery.

I WENT ON to middle school, high school, and college. I became a father and launched my comic career. But I never forgot Miss Avery.

I remembered how at first I couldn't stand her, and then how I slowly realized that Miss Avery's tough talk was a form of tough love. It was a way to get us to appreciate our education and to work hard to get the most out of it, so that we could create opportunities in our lives. The kind of focus and skills that I once lacked, and that are so critical in my career and family today, I first gained in Miss Avery's class. I'd never loved math, for instance, but I began to see the magic in numbers in the sixth grade, and I became comfortable enough that more than thirty years later, I can check the accuracy of my own books and make sure nobody is ripping me off.

Miss Avery could also be an undercover softie. I know that some of my classmates didn't have much money, but somehow we were all able to go on field trips to the circus and the fair. I know now that Miss Avery was going into her pocket to make that happen. And I remember when some kids didn't have lunch money, Miss Avery would pay for their meals.

I started talking about her on the radio, how she would pull out toothpaste to keep a kid from being teased for having bad breath, and how she motivated us to study math, history, and English, and to enjoy doing it.

So, about twenty-five years after I'd graduated from sixth grade, I decided I was going to find Miss Avery. By now, my friend Roosevelt—who'd also been in Miss Avery's class—was working for me as a security guard and assistant.

"Hey, Ro," I said one day, "let's go to Miss Avery's house."

Now, neither of us had ever been to Miss Avery's house. But I figured that her phone number was still listed, like most older people's numbers in Birmingham back then. And when we were in the sixth grade and she would be fussing at us, or lecturing while she stood at the blackboard, we'd mumble, "Shut up, Alene," under our breath—so we knew her first name.

Sure enough, I was able to track down where she lived without too much trouble, and Roosevelt and I just showed up at her house one day.

When Miss Avery opened that door, she was a little grayer and a lot older. But she grabbed and hugged me like I was her long-lost child. It turns out that she had followed my career and even listened to me on the radio, with all the hip-hop, prank calls, and crazy jokes, because she was proud that her former student had done well.

She invited me in and offered me a glass of water or a Sprite. I said yes and waited for her as she went to a little freezer set up in her dining room and pulled out a bag of ice, saying over her shoulder that her ice maker wasn't working.

I asked her what was wrong with the ice maker, and as she started rambling out an explanation, I decided to take a look around. "She's a retired schoolteacher," I thought to myself. "Why doesn't she have a working ice maker?"

This woman had to be in her seventies. She had encouraged us to study and gone into her own pocket to make sure we could have fun at the fair, or just have something to eat. There was no way I was going to let her sit up in a hot house with no ice.

I asked her for a pen and paper. "Miss Avery, I'm about to walk around your house and see what you need."

She was embarrassed and said I didn't have to do all that, but I ignored her and made a checklist anyway.

Let's just say her living conditions weren't where I wanted them to be. I thought that was unacceptable for a woman who had done so much for me, and all the other students who made their way through her classroom. I told her to pack a bag.

I rented a hotel room, where Miss Avery stayed for about two weeks, and I pretty much remodeled her whole house. I bought her a brand-new refrigerator, got her kitchen floor redone, and installed new carpet. I put $1,000 on her J. C. Penney credit card so she could pick out curtains and other furniture that reflected her tastes. And I bought her a recliner, where she could kick back as she listened to me on the radio.

We kept visiting. At first, it was just Ro and me, stopping by for thirty minutes. Then we would sit around laughing for a couple of hours. When I discovered that she and D'essence had the same birthday, I started taking the kids by her house. She became a surrogate grandmother. I mean, we felt so at home that I would take a nap on the couch, my kids would be spread out on the floor, and Miss Avery would just sit there watching *The Price Is Right*. Miss Avery had some beautiful nephews and nieces in Chicago and Cleveland, but she'd never had kids of her own, so she was appreciative and happy to have the Smiley bunch, her new family, dropping by all the time.

Every year, I put her on a plane so that she could travel to her family reunions. She flew first class, and I arranged to have a wheelchair carry her to and from the gate. Her nieces and nephews, to whom I remain close, said she would arrive at the reunion and boast to everyone about how her student Broderick had flown her into town.

Back in Birmingham, Ro would pick up Miss Avery once a month and bring her to my home for Sunday dinner. I'd always make collard greens and chicken and dumplings, because she loved them. And she was the only person I ever allowed to smoke in my house. She'd pull out a Salem 100 cigarette after dinner, and in between puffs, she'd sip a glass of Courvoisier and Coke.

"Can you believe this, Miss Avery?" I'd say, while Ro sat nearby. "Two of the worst kids in your sixth-grade class are now your primary caretakers." She'd blow some smoke and burst out laughing.

It was great to see Miss Avery so relaxed. When she wasn't cracking on our mothers in the sixth grade, she spoke very formally. You know the type—"Two tutors tooted the flute and then they flew down the chute." But all that stiff talk went out the window after she'd had a couple of drinks and a good meal.

And do you know what else? Sometimes Ms. Hanks, my old elementary school principal and Miss Avery's friend, would join us. Ms. Hanks was still in principal mode, and she didn't drink or smoke. But the three of us would tell old stories and have a great time. If you had told eleven-year-old Rickey Smiley that he would be hanging out with his mean old teacher and the principal who used to literally beat his butt, he would have told you that you were out of your mind. But there we were.

For about four wonderful years, I took care of Miss Avery. I paid for a gardener to keep her lawn cut, and I gave her $150 a week to pay for her prescription medications, so that she could spend her social security check on what she wanted and not what she needed. She had become so integrated into my world that she was going to be on my reality show. She actually shot the pilot with me and my family back in 2015, and the producers thought she was hilarious. The whole world was about to get a taste of Miss Avery.

One Friday, Miss Avery called me and said that she was having pain in one of her feet, and she was going to see the doctor on Monday. Her niece Betty McLaney, who happened to live down the street from my grandparents, was going to take her.

I was headed to Minneapolis to do a show, but I told her that when I got back, I'd head straight to her doctor's office. I wanted to ask him some questions about what was going on with her foot. She said that would be fine.

I went to Minneapolis, did my show, and then headed back to my hotel room. My head had just hit the pillow when my phone rang. I glanced at it and saw that it was Miss Avery calling. But I was so sleepy. I figured I would just call her back in the morning.

The next day, I flew into Atlanta, and from there I was going to be driven back to Birmingham. Not long after I landed, my mother called. I answered and got the bad news.

"I just wanted you to know that Miss Avery passed away in her sleep," she said.

Right now, thinking about that gut punch of a call, my eyes are welling up. But before now, I never cried over Miss Avery. I think it's because I knew that the last few years of her life, I had given Miss Avery my all.

Her funeral was held on a beautiful Saturday morning in the summer. When it was my turn to speak about her, I went up to the microphone and I told the mourners all the funny stories—how she was the first and only teacher I ever had who talked about my mother; how she'd stomp in those "yo-yo" shoes until it looked like they were about to crack; how she'd pack you off to the bathroom in a minute to brush your teeth and get yourself together.

Mourners in the pews started cracking up. You would have thought it was one of my comedy shows instead of a funeral. It was a celebration.

When I would go on the road, Miss Avery used to call me often. That woman would sing at the drop of a dime.

"Jesus is realllll." I would put the phone on speaker and let her rich alto voice fill the hotel room.

On my phone, I still have a clip of her singing her heart out.

Before the funeral service, I had asked the attendants to connect my phone to the church's speakers. When I finished talking, Miss Avery's voice filled that church—her church—for the last time.

"Jesus is reallllll. For I can feel him in my soul."

The church got quiet for a moment. Then, when they began to roll out the casket, and everyone stood to walk out, the mourners began to sing.

"Jesus is realll. For I can feel him in my soul."

There are people who have an impact on your life. They give you an opportunity. They recommend you for a job. They teach you what you need to know. They bring you to the party, or give you the knowledge you need to make the most of that experience whenever you arrive.

Never forget those who've been there for you. Drop a good word for an old friend. Lend a little time to the elder who steered you the right way. Look up and thank one of your most impactful teachers. Reach out to the one who brought you to the party, and then dance, dance, dance.

THAT'S SHOWBIZ

We live in a world that encourages envy. There's always a commercial showing you what product you need to buy or a reality show telling you how you need to live. Buy this car, and it will change your life! Try this diet, and whittle yourself down to happiness! Wear this brand, and you'll attract whomever your heart desires.

And if you don't buy it, don't try it, don't want it, then what the heck is wrong with you?

All that chatter can make it hard to figure out what you are really looking for, to hear that inner voice that lets you know what is truly right for you. Why should you buy a Mercedes if you prefer the glide of a Mini Cooper? Why enroll in nursing school if you'd rather write computer code? Why go out to that club when you'd prefer to just stay at home and stream Pandora?

I'm not saying that you shouldn't have goals, but they should reflect the aspirations you feel deep in your bones—not the boxes that someone else tells you to tick off. You're going to have to live in whatever space you create, so you want to make sure that space is where you want to be.

Falling in step with the crowd without thinking has led a whole lot of people to bankruptcy court—or to the graveyard. What God has for you is for you. It may take a while to get to it, but it's there, waiting for the right moment to manifest in your life. What's been ordered up by a higher power can't be borrowed or stolen by anybody else.

That also means that what God has for the guy living in the bigger house up the hill is meant for him. And it's not right or productive to spend time thinking about how he got it, why he got it, and why you're not the one sitting in that home theater instead of him.

Besides, you don't know what's going on behind your neighbor's closed doors. He could be catching hell up in that house. He may be struggling to pay that mortgage, or having so much trouble with his kids that he can't sleep at night. Whatever is going on, the good things and the bad, are ultimately his business. Not yours or anybody else's.

I make my living in a field where success is front and center. My peers are onstage. They're making movies and starring in their own television shows. All that celebrity, and the money that can flow with it, can be intoxicating. Applause may still be echoing in your ears when you put your head down on the pillow at night. You can get caught up in the chase for the next award, the next show, the next big contract, the next dollar bill.

There are plenty of perks that come with fame—if you like getting to cut the line at a show, grabbing an impossible reservation, or getting your ego stroked twenty-four hours a day, seven days a week.

But I will also tell you that there are many things that are far more important than fame and wealth, things that you can't buy at Saks Fifth Avenue or order from Amazon. A good life has peace and balance. No amount of gold is worth more.

MY CLIMB IN the comedy business started off slow but steady.

I'd had a lot of different jobs, selling shoes, baking pizzas, trimming shrubs. But none made me feel like I did when I performed at the Comedy Club's open mic night. When I was on that stage, the adrenaline rushed through me. I felt like I was just beginning to understand something that I could one day master. I felt a comfort that let me know that this is where I needed to be.

I was an education major at Alabama State, but I was taking my sweet time earning my degree. My commitment to academics was nowhere near as strong as my interest in football, frat parties, and fraternizing with the ladies.

I pledged Omega Psi Phi and had a ball hanging out in the quad that we called "the yard." On the weekends, I was traveling to step shows and sharpening up new, young pledges who wanted to join the brotherhood of purple and gold.

I eventually transferred to Miles College, where I planned to finish earning the credits to get my bachelor of arts degree. But after I started doing comedy, I knew that I was done with school. Comedy was what I wanted to do, and I had to make it work. So in 1990, I dropped out of Miles and focused on my career full-time.

Since I didn't host at the Comedy Club every weekend, I kept on playing piano at churches around Birmingham and pursuing my own gigs to make end's meet.

No job was too small. Many weekends, I performed at reunions or the family get-togethers of my friends. I'd stand in front of somebody's fireplace without a microphone and riff for ten or fifteen minutes. I remember how one time, my friend Rolanda Hollis hired me to perform at her parents' anniversary party. I got paid $150.

It could be a birthday party, a renewal of wedding vows, a christening. It didn't matter; I was just glad to be there. I thought every one of those appearances in someone's living room or backyard was as big a deal as a show at the Laugh Factory in New York City. It was a chance for me to try out material and to hand out my phone number to a wider circle of people who might be interested in booking me.

After standing in front of a mantel crowded with Junior's senior prom pictures and making Grandma Phyllis or Uncle Chuck laugh a little bit, I would usually meet a couple of people who wanted me to perform at an office party or maybe an event at their club.

I'd tacked a calendar to a wall in my apartment. When I got home, I would dutifully take out a pencil, stand in front of the calendar, and fill in those little squares with all of my upcoming gigs. Each mark I made, each joke I told, represented a little bit of progress. And the $75 or $100 I got added up at the end of the month, especially when I tossed in the $75 I would make playing piano at church.

More often than not, the crowd at those small gatherings was predominantly black. I bring that up because at the Comedy Club, where I entertained larger crowds, my audience tended to be white.

Now, the same type of humor doesn't work for everybody. A crowd at the Statehouse Convention Center in Little Rock may not have the same idea of what's funny as the folks at a club on Los Angeles's Sunset Strip. Folks in my grandparents' generation, who grew up watching Milton Berle or Redd Foxx, may not relate to the same humor as their great-grandchildren who love *The Daily Show* and Trevor Noah.

One night in 1992, I found out the hard way that the jokes that typically cracked up a white crowd at an upscale Birmingham club weren't going to work with an auditorium full of black teenagers ready to hear some hip-hop.

I had started gaining a reputation around town, so I'd gotten booked to be the comic relief at a concert at the Birmingham-Jefferson Civic Center. The pay was only fifty dollars, but the exposure was significant, because the show was basically the World Series of gangster rap. Ice Cube, who'd left N.W.A and become a superstar on his own, was a headliner. So was the Oakland rapper Too Short, along with the Geto Boys, who were straight out of Houston's Fifth Ward and had blown up the charts with "Mind Playing Tricks on Me."

Before I'd even opened my mouth, I knew that I was a fish out of water. Wearing my glossy, buttoned-up, going-to-Bible-study suit, I walked out in front of a gin-and-juice-sipping audience that was decked out in T-shirts and jeans.

It got worse fast. My first joke included an impression of Ronald Reagan.

It doesn't matter what my second joke was. Nobody could hear it over all the booing.

"Get your a-- off the stage and bring up Ice Cube!" people yelled out.

The ten minutes I stood on that stage felt like a whole year. A decade later, Ice Cube would hire me to play a fake, thieving Santa Claus in *Friday After Next*, the third film in his popular *Friday* franchise. But that night, when I walked backstage, he laughed at me like he was the most popular kid at school and I was the playground misfit. But embarrassing moments can teach you things. Painful moments can put you on notice. I had to come up with some jokes that a young black audience might laugh at. I needed to do a better job tapping into the black experience.

I needed to talk about church. I needed to talk about grandmothers who helped raise their grandchildren and were the center of the extended family. I needed to talk about being broke in an economy where the playing field wasn't always level. I had to get with it.

I went back to my apartment and started writing. I had a few set jokes to build on, like the frame of a house that still needs the drywall, the doors, and the shutters. I started cobbling together a new, more Afrocentric routine. And it wasn't long before I saw an opportunity to try it out.

When I introduced headliners at the Comedy Club, I'd get to tell only a couple of jokes before I needed to bring the big acts up and hurry myself off the stage. But on Saturdays, before the last show of the night, Bruce would sometimes give lesser-known comics the chance to perform a longer routine before the headliner came back out to perform.

WENN-FM, a local R & B station that was owned by a prominent black businessman named A. G. Gaston, was taking over the Comedy Club for an evening. It was going to be the one night that the club was guaranteed to be filled with an African-American audience. And who was the headliner? Steve Harvey.

By then, Steve was hosting *Showtime at the Apollo,* which had made his popularity explode. Every black person in Birmingham who could fit in the Comedy Club was going to show up, including owners of other venues, radio personalities, and concert promoters. You don't know how badly I wanted to be the one warming up that audience for Steve.

But as in every other part of life, from the play at your elementary school to the deacon board at church, politics were involved. I wasn't the only one who wanted a chance to be up on that stage. One of the Comedy Club's waiters was also an up-and-coming comedian. Since he was regularly waiting tables, he was obviously there a lot more than I was, and Bruce liked him. He and I, however, didn't get along.

I'd heard that he talked about me behind my back to the waitresses and other folks working at the club. He'd put me down, saying that I wasn't funny. I could tell after a while that his negativity was rubbing off on some of the other club employees. They just weren't as friendly anymore. And while they joked and laughed with him, they'd get quiet when I came around.

I wanted to confront that guy and curse him out, but I had to stay focused. I didn't want to get labeled a troublemaker and potentially mess up my relationship with Bruce, which was more important. That time, taking the high road didn't get me my shot. Bruce chose the other guy to open for Steve.

I was angry. I felt like I'd been undermined and that all of that guy's trash-talking and getting the club's staff on his side had paid off in his favor. But when I eventually calmed down, the lessons I'd learned from my grandfather Ernest, from all of my uncles, from my peewee football coaches, started to kick in. I'd been knocked down. Now I had to figure out a way to get back up.

On WENN night, Steve's second set was going to start at twelve a.m. I set my alarm for just before midnight and took a short nap. When the buzzer rang, I got up, lit a couple of candles for ambiance like I was Benjamin Franklin, and sat at my kitchen table with the determination to write jokes until Steve's set was over and folks were walking out the Comedy Club's doors. I wrote every line, every scenario that I could think of that was funny. I had chosen to start writing at the time Steve took the stage not only to keep me from obsessing over my lost opportunity, but to set a vow that not only would I one day be an opening act for Steve, but one day I'd be the headliner at that club and sell that room out.

I had two notebooks where I sketched dozens of stories, and then a third where I wrote final, more polished versions, as if I were back in school working on an English essay.

Long past the Comedy Club's closing time, I was scribbling down ideas. That night, I can honestly say that I wrote some of the funniest skits I'd created up to that point. I look at that evening, when I sat hunched over a table with those candles burning, as a turning point in my career.

I'd found a way to channel my anger. It's fine to feel mad for a moment, but you can't stay there. Your anger won't alter the course of the person you're mad at, but it can definitely throw you off track. Anger distracts you. It takes you off of your game. I had to make my anger mean something, to let it lead somewhere positive. Instead of stewing, I let my rage motivate me and charge up my creativity.

I swear, the next time I hit the stage, I was funny at a whole different level. I could feel it. The audience could feel it. I think that waiter and Bruce felt it, too.

I WAS ON a mission. I was hungry. Instead of just bouncing between the Comedy Club and people's living rooms, I started performing in restaurants. Other comedians would share information about out-of-town bars and grills that had their own comedy nights, so maybe on a Wednesday, I'd head to an Applebee's in Montgomery. They'd have a microphone set up in a corner. I'd perform, pocket $150, and drive the ninety-one miles right back home to Birmingham, because I didn't have any money for a hotel room. I spent about four or five years playing every Red Robin, Applebee's, and Fuddruckers within a hundred-mile radius.

I also started getting bookings at music venues around Birmingham. There was a club, the French Quarter, with a house band called the French Connection, where I began performing a few nights a week. I went on between the band's sets. This audience really just wanted to listen to music, so to make them laugh, my timing had to be precise, and my jokes had to be on point.

The French Quarter had an African-American clientele, and I was still polishing a routine that would really fire up that audience. Lenora Spencer, the French Connection's female vocalist, and the band's bass guitarist, whom we called Pim, would actually give me jokes to try out onstage.

I looked at every performance as a test and every person who gave me a chance to perform as a teacher. I took Lenora's and Pim's jokes, and of course improvised my own. I took mental notes on which riffs coaxed more laughs from the crowd, and which ones fell flat.

But there was one person in the club whom I could never move. He was the band's main vocalist, Irvin Abercrombie. He would never laugh at my jokes. And I mean never.

The French Connection would open for great acts like jazz pianist Alex Bugnon and the famous smooth-jazz saxophonist Jerome Najee Rasheed, better known as Najee. They were that good. I remember one night, the French Connection was singing "Can't Stop" by the popular R & B group After 7. They had the crowd up on its feet. When the band finally took a break, I had to go on that stage and try to make those folks laugh, when they were sweating, breathing hard, and just wanted to dance some more. But that was another teachable moment, and I did pretty well.

After my act, Lenora, Pim, and their other bandmates patted me on the back and told me good job. But Irvin was just standing there, stone-faced.

"You will never be able to make me laugh," he said, giving me a hard stare.

All the rest of the time, Irvin was incredibly nice to me, so I was a little puzzled about why he was always so hard on my act. But I quickly realized what he was doing. He was challenging me. He was pushing me. "Try harder. Get better. Be funnier" was his unspoken message.

I never did make him laugh. But his tough-loving attitude helped me to up my game, so that every other person sitting in that club's audience did laugh.

I kept casting my net wider and wider. Bruce Ayers had been instrumental in helping me kick off my career, but there was a whole fraternity of local black club owners who helped me to find my swagger.

Michael McMillan owned the French Quarter. A guy named Mr. T owned a place called T's. And Mr. Thurman owned the Speakeasy. Each of them encouraged me, and by giving me work, they helped me to hone my craft and grow my reputation.

Finally, in 1997, I got a permanent, regular gig. There was a new black comedy club opening up called the Cobblestone, named for the pebbly street where it was located. A lady from Chicago named Lois Eiacher put up the money, and another businesswoman, Tiffini Swain, managed it. I was going to earn $300 a week, a small fortune in my eyes, which would go a long way toward helping me take care of my young son Brandon.

The Cobblestone was a laboratory for me. Performing at least five shows every single week for about a year and a half made me damn good. That regular routine, each time in front of a new, different crowd, gave me the final preparation I needed. Soon, when I got my shot to appear on BET's *Comic View*, I was able to target my jokes like a marksman on a shooting range. That first *Comic View* appearance would pave the way for me to eventually host *Comic View* in 2000, and then to host it again in 2004.

My radio career also began to kick into gear. I approached WENN, to see if they'd consider featuring a comedian on the air, but the station's management wasn't interested. Another opportunity soon emerged.

I had a childhood friend, Corey White, who'd recently started working as a part-time disc jockey at WBHJ, or 95.7 Jamz, a new station based in Tuscaloosa. He said that the station managers might want a comedian on their new morning show, and I should think about auditioning.

Corey turned out to be yet another one of the many wonderful people who did me a huge favor out of the goodness of his heart, putting me on a path that would change my life. He introduced me to the station's program director, Mickey Johnson, who, along with the general manager, David DuBose, took a chance on me and gave me my first turn at a radio mic. Two decades later, Nicky still programs that station, and Corey is its operations manager.

Every day, from Monday through Friday, I would drive sixty miles from Birmingham to Tuscaloosa to do the morning show, which started at five a.m. Then I'd turn around and drive back home. Initially, it was really more like an internship, because for the first four or five months, I didn't get paid. When I did start earning a paycheck, it added up to only $16,000 a year.

But I was patient. I figured the bigger money would come later. I needed to learn and grow, and I'd never been afraid of hard work. Plus, the exposure and experience I was gaining at WBHJ was helping bring more money to the table. I was getting my name out to a broader audience. I became the first choice to host concerts, Greek step shows, and other events at the University of Alabama, because people wanted to hire "that guy who was on the radio."

And it was at WBHJ that I perfected a routine that added a whole new dimension to my career—prank calls.

Before Tammi Mac and Chris Coleman joined the station, the morning show featured the personalities Africa, Buck Wilde, and me. I was a big fan of the Jerky Boys, these crazy guys who would call people up, pretend to be someone else, and practically give the person on the receiving end a heart attack.

Buck Wilde loved prank calls, too, but at the time, they were more popular with the white DJs at the classic rock or country-western stations. We were spinning hip-hop, but Buck suggested that we shake up our show and start putting prank calls into the mix.

One of the first prank calls I made was to a lady named Miss May Lee. Her son had stopped by the station and told me about how she'd gone up to a school and gotten into an argument with some kids and their parents. So I called her while we were on the air and pretended to be one of those schoolchildren's grandparents.

Boy, Miss May Lee laid me out. I thought she was going to come through the receiver and wring my neck. We were both sweating by the time I finally told her that I was Rickey Smiley at WBHJ, and she'd just been pranked. To this day, I still run into people who remember that call, and it turned out to be the spark that really set off my prank-calling career. It made those routines one of my signatures.

Things began to go into overdrive. I had done *Def Comedy Jam* five years before, and while I was at WBHJ, I had gotten the chance to open for the Kings of Comedy tour. At the Cobblestone, I was onstage for a couple of shows on Friday, a couple of shows on Saturday, and at least one show every Sunday for almost two years. I was well into my groove.

I developed a character named Ms. Bernice Jenkins, who was a combination of my grandmothers and every crotchety, loving older woman I'd ever known. I also had another idea.

Remember that little boy in church who could never quite learn his Easter speech? He'd stand there struggling, and his mother or the Sunday school teacher would stand on the side trying to help him, while the other kids waiting in the wings would strain not to burst out laughing. Meanwhile, all of their parents would be giving them the evil eye and mouthing what they'd do to them if they let out one giggle.

I drew on that experience to create a new character. I knew how he would speak, how he would walk, and what he would look like, down to his thick pair of Coke bottle–lensed glasses. I wanted to take him to the stage. But he needed a name.

Cedric the Entertainer was a great friend and mentor I'd met through Steve Harvey. We were in my car riding one day when I told him about this new character I'd cooked up.

Cedric listened, thought a second, then blurted out, "Call him Little Darryl." And so Lil Darryl was born.

The first time I tried out Lil Darryl in front of an audience, I went to this hole-in-the-wall club that was rough. It was where pimps, dope dealers, and strippers hung out, and if they didn't think you were funny, they'd shake their keys at you, basically shaking you up and eventually shaking your behind right off the stage. I'd only been performing for about a minute when they started reaching in their pockets and purses. Then I pulled out Lil Darryl.

He was the last model in my fictitious church fashion show. When he finished doing his pitiful sashay, I stepped off the stage like it was a real runway and walked right out the club's front door.

Those folks in the club were laughing so hard, you could hear tables and chairs being turned over and people screaming inside. I walked back in to the roar of applause.

The next time I played Lil Darryl, it was a few months later, and I was appearing on *Comic View*.

It was 1998. *Comic View* only paid $150, which the people who ran that network eventually took a lot of flak for, but we comedians were just happy for the opportunity. It was the chance to perform before a national audience and share the stage with the funniest dudes and ladies in the business.

That $150 didn't even cover plane fare from Alabama to California, so I had to scrape together the money to fly Brandon and myself to Los Angeles. The great thing is that there was a brotherhood and sisterhood of comics who could help make all the ends meet, for example by letting you stay at their place instead of a hotel you couldn't afford.

Just like Omega Psi Phi has its chapters—Alpha Phi in Birmingham, Kappa Beta in Holly Springs, Mississippi—each major city had its crew of comedians. In Chicago, there were George Willborn and Tony Sculfield. Atlanta was home turf for Earthquake and Bruce Bruce. New York had A. G. White and my good friend J. B. Smoove. And in Los Angeles, you had dudes like Tommy Davidson, who starred on *In Living Color* and was one of my all-time idols, along with my great friend Pierre.

We all looked out for one another. Each of us had his own style, and each city might have had its own unique regional inflection, but as surprising as it may sound, there wasn't jealousy or rivalry between us. We understood that we were playing in a tough game, and we supported one another's aspirations. We felt there was room for each of us at the top, and we wanted all of us to get there.

Pierre, one of the funniest comics on the circuit, let Brandon and me sleep at his house when I traveled out there to appear on BET. I get emotional thinking about it, because nobody has to let you stay at their house. Nobody has to drive through all of that Los Angeles traffic to Los Angeles International Airport to pick up your child and you. Nobody has to drive you to the BET taping when they could just show you to the bus stop. But Pierre did all of that for me, and it wasn't the first time.

The day of the BET taping, I was part of the group of comics that was performing last, along with Katt Williams, who at that time went by the name Alley Cat. We'd been taping all day, and the audience was beat. Nobody was really laughing. Mike Epps hit the stage right before me.

I remember that Mike was wearing a Dallas Cowboys jersey. When he finished his set, he passed me backstage.

"Just play to the camera, man," he advised. "That audience is dead."

I knew that success happens when preparation meets opportunity. I had been performing my act at the Cobblestone a few nights every week, and I had the timing as precise as a Swiss watch. I was ready to wake that crowd up. And when I walked out there and did Lil Darryl, it was fire. The audience just exploded. I brought straight heat.

Zooman, who's become one of the most popular comedians in the country, was in his trailer watching my performance on a small monitor. I'd known him since we did *Def Comedy Jam* almost a decade before, and we'd been good friends ever since. He was also an integral part of the comic brotherhood.

When I finished performing, I walked backstage. I saw Zooman coming toward me. He had a strange look on his face.

"Oh my God," he said.

I was wondering if I had done something wrong. Did I accidentally curse on national television?

"Oh my God."

Did I come down too hard on somebody in the audience? What was wrong?

Then Zooman grabbed me and lifted me up.

"Man, it's over!"

"What?" I asked.

"Your career! You snapped! You killed it! Your whole life is fixing to change, bro."

Then Mike, Katt, and all the other comedians started running toward me. They were hugging me, slapping me on my back, giving me high fives. You would have thought I had hit the winning home run in the World Series. It was like I was running into home base, and all those comics were standing there, waiting to celebrate and carry me on their shoulders.

They felt it. They knew it. Lil Darryl made me famous.

The first thing I did after that was to stop driving to all my gigs. Before that, I'd been staying in Super 8s and Motel 6s, or sleeping on a friend's floor. Every once in a while, a club owner would have a cousin who had a spare bedroom, and that's where I'd spend the night after a show. But now all that was over.

If you wanted me to perform, you had to book and pay for my travel. I wanted round-trip first-class tickets, and since I don't like hotels much to begin with, any room you reserved needed to be a five-star property.

My pay had been steadily rising since I'd done *Def Comedy Jam* in 1992, when I'd gone from earning $150 to $500 or $1,000 a performance. But after I debuted Lil Darryl to the world on BET, my pay skyrocketed. I was getting $5,000, then $15,000, then $20,000 a show. I left 95.7 in late 1998 and just toured full-time. Not too long after, I would be able to command up to six figures for doing a couple hours of comedy.

I'd recorded all the prank phone calls I'd ever done on the radio, and when I was on the road, wherever I performed, I sold them on tapes and compact discs. I had about six volumes, and I would stand in the lobby after a show and autograph every last one of them.

By the time I hosted *Comic View* in 2000, I was getting my first real taste of fame, the kind where people randomly recognized me when I went to the movies, walked through the airport, or even just tried to grab some takeout at a drive-through window.

When I wanted a milkshake or Egg McMuffin from McDonald's, I started learning how to disguise myself. Because if I didn't, Precious, working at the window, would get excited and get my order all wrong. I'd keep my window half rolled up and my baseball cap pulled low, and Precious was none the wiser.

I found out that I had some famous fans, as well.

Eddie Murphy had been one of the cast members on *Saturday Night Live* in the early 1980s, and his sketches and impressions of characters like James Brown and Buckwheat launched him into super-stardom. He had blockbuster films like *Trading Places* and *Beverly Hills Cop*. He was one of the biggest stars in the world, and yet his humor was pure Brooklyn—raw, down-to-earth, and hilarious.

The comic Earthquake had told me that Eddie thought I was funny, but I just brushed that off. It seemed impossible that Eddie Murphy had even heard of me. Then one day I was in the car, heading to Mississippi to do a show, when my cell phone rang. Believe it or not, it was Eddie Murphy on the line.

"Yo, man, where are you?" he said.

"Who is this?"

"It's Eddie. Eddie Murphy." His voice was unmistakable. I sat there in disbelief. "Are you out here, in LA? Where you at? Alabama?"

"Uh, yeah," I stammered back. "Well, I'm heading to a show in Mississippi right now."

"Man, you are funny!" he said. I'd won a BET comedy award one year, and Eddie remembered. He told me that he was proud of me and to take care. And that was it. I was in a state of shock but happy.

Then, on one of my next visits to Los Angeles, I finally got to meet him.

Eddie had heard I would be in town and called to invite me to his home. I was staying at the Sofitel, and about six p.m. one evening, the comedian and actor Miguel Nunez Jr. arrived to pick me up.

I got in the car, and we drove to the Hollywood Hills, straight to the giant gate at the entrance to Eddie Murphy's house.

I felt like I was stepping into Shangri-la. Well, Shangri-la if ambrosia was soul food.

You would think Eddie Murphy would have some fancy chef, but instead he hosted a down-home spread. I'm talking macaroni and cheese, collard greens, corn bread, and barbecue chicken. Somebody had baked a pound cake with chocolate icing, and there was even a pot of pig ears boiling in Eddie Murphy's kitchen.

And what did we have to wash it all down with? Kool-Aid.

Eddie greeted me, then offered to give me a tour of his palatial house. Afterward, he took me back to the kitchen, asked if I was hungry, and told me to make myself a plate.

I recognized a few people I had met before in Dallas, and Eddie was so warm, it felt like I was just hanging around with some old buddies back home. Later, we all watched a movie, or rather the movie watched me—because I was so full and happy that I fell asleep.

There was just one person, whose name isn't worth remembering, who messed up the vibe. When everyone was standing around chatting and laughing, he rolled up beside me. "Hey, man, while you're over here, you ought to talk to Eddie about any idea you have for a show or a film."

I looked at him like he had lost his mind, and I shut him down quickly. "No," I said. "Because he didn't invite me over here for that."

If Eddie Murphy called me again one day and asked me to be in a movie, that would be great. But if he didn't, having his friendship mattered more to me than a role in *Beverly Hills Cop 15*. The way Eddie treated me that night, welcoming me into his home, introducing me to his friends, sharing his home cooking, I felt I didn't need one other thing from him in life. Not everything has to be a transaction. A gesture of kindness and camaraderie can be enough.

I WAS MAKING so much money on the road that I was able to move out of my town house and buy a large, comfortable home in the suburbs of Birmingham. And around 2001, I experienced being on a syndicated radio show for the first time. The radio personality Doug Banks wanted a nationally known comic to join his program, and he asked me to come on board. He was based in Dallas, but the show was syndicated in at least a dozen other markets, including New York, Chicago, and Jacksonville. It was a sweet deal, since I was able to be on the air every day and tape right from my hometown. It wasn't necessary for me to be in Texas, since I wasn't the show's host.

That gig lasted a couple of years—until I got fired.

The first issue was that the morning producer and I didn't get along well. He would try to tell me what to say on the air. "Hey, Rickey, try this joke!"

I have news for you—never try to tell somebody who is funny for a living what funny is. If you haven't stood on a stage telling jokes, if you've never read the mood of an audience, if you've never had to stand your ground when the heckling starts, you don't have any business offering tips on a routine.

But what actually got me kicked off the show was the way I was perceived in New York City. From what other people told me, the program director there just wasn't a fan of my Southern-style humor.

It wasn't personal. It was business. If you have a show that is syndicated in New York, that is always going to be your number one, most
important market, and so the people running that operation have got
to be happy. They weren't, so they had to let me go. But Doug was a
true gentleman. Darryl Brown, an executive from ABC Radio, gave me
a nice severance check, and he told me how much he liked me. And
my entertainment attorney, Rickey Anderson, reassured me that things
like this happened all the time.

It was a little jarring, but I took it in stride. Anyway, my bread and
butter was on the road. And, as fate would have it, radio came calling
again within a year.

One day, my attorney told me to expect a call from Steve Harvey
around noon.

It was the call when Steve told me that he had gotten a radio deal
with the company Clear Channel and that he had recommended to his
bosses at Radio One that I take over his show on KBFB-FM in Dallas.

I was reluctant to leave behind my life in Birmingham, but the next
day, with butterflies in my stomach, I got on a Southwest jet, because I
felt that I couldn't jeopardize my relationship with Steve, especially
when he had stuck his neck out for me yet again.

I sat in the back row of that plane and worried all the way to Texas.
When I landed, a driver met me at the airport, and we went straight to
the Red Bird Mall, where Steve was doing a radio event. Then we
hopped back in the limousine and went to a spot called JJ Fish, to pick
up some lunch. I wasn't that hungry, to tell you the truth, but I was glad
for the distraction of chowing down on fish and French fries, because I
was nervous. I had just won custody of Brandon, and I didn't know
much about Dallas. I wasn't sure that I could make a job in Dallas work.

Still, I was always excited to be around Steve, and I put on a good
front. He said that the next day, I was going to meet with the program

director and general manager to talk about the potential job. I gulped and said okay.

The next morning, I went to the station and appeared on the morning show as Steve's guest. When we got off the air, I met Sean Nun, the general manager, who is one of the most supportive radio executives I've ever encountered, and John Candeleera, the program director. We called him John Candy, like the famous comedian from *Planes, Trains and Automobiles*. My attorney, Rickey Anderson, was also there.

John and Sean asked what kind of ideas I had for the morning show, and I just spoke from my heart. I said I wanted to do things to help uplift the community. Back in Birmingham, radio was a cornerstone, offering education as well as communion. On the less serious side, I also wanted to continue my prank calls and to host events outside the station that we could broadcast, like sketch shows and karaoke.

They liked what I had to say and they told me that I had the job. Just like that. I flew right back to Birmingham, in a daze but excited. Alfred Liggins, the station's CEO, called me the next day, so that we could negotiate my salary.

I had to move fast. I had bought my mother and stepfather a home and asked them to keep Brandon on the days that I was away. Steve was so kind that he did some initial shows with me, before my program officially launched. He wanted to help me get acclimated. Our chemistry was so strong that I started to question the idea of hosting my own morning show in Dallas. I suggested that I go to New York with him to become part of *The Steve Harvey Morning Show*.

I even talked to Rushion McDonald, Steve's manager, about it. But Rushion knew that while Steve and I made a good team, I was also hesitating to have my own platform out of fear. Dallas was a bigger pond than Birmingham, and I was a little nervous about whether or not I could carry all that on my own. Rushion was like Steve, and like

Irvin Abercrombie in that band I used to open for. He was pushing me. He was challenging me.

"You're a strong personality," he said. "It's time for you to leave the nest. You need to have your own morning show."

Do you know that Steve, Rushion, and I literally had a fight about it? We argued like three old men back in the day, debating who was the better baseball player, Joe DiMaggio or Satchel Paige.

Finally Rushion yelled, "You've got to look at the big picture, Rickey! You've got an opportunity to take over radio."

Then Steve shut it down. "Look, Rickey," he said, "if this situation doesn't work out, you can come to New York, and I'll create a spot for you on my show." That sounded all right to me.

Three days later, *The Rickey Smiley Morning Show* hit the air.

Now I needed to build my crew, the cast that would sit beside me day after day and help me entertain an audience. The first to join me was Lester Raynel Ruffin, who is known as Headkrack. Then a week later came Rocky Turner, whose stage name is Rock-T. And eventually Gary Hayes, otherwise known as Gary with da Tea, also became part of our team. I'd met Gary with da Tea through Steve. He had delivered the gossip and horoscopes on Steve's show. Initially, he wasn't on air with me. He was more of an assistant. He has a flamboyant on-air personality, but Gary is one of the savviest, most organized and professional people I've ever met. He helped me find an apartment and buy my furniture, and even made sure my bills were paid.

After about a year, I talked to Gary about possibly joining my show. When he did, it was like I'd laid out a jigsaw puzzle and just hadn't been able to finish it, but now I'd located the missing piece. We were in perfect harmony.

Next came Juicy. I was a fan of shock jock Howard Stern, who featured a little person named Hank on his show. I wanted my cast to be inclusive, too. I had an acquaintance who told me that there was a little lady who had been in Shelly Garrett's popular play *Beauty Shop*. My friend was reluctant to introduce us, though, because she thought I might tease her and be a little mean. It took a whole year for her to bring Juicy by the studio.

When she did, we were brother and sister from the beginning. She walked in the door, we took one look at each other, and then we both burst out laughing.

"What's your name?" I asked her.

"Shirlene," she said in her squeak of a voice. "But you can call me Juicy."

I offered her a job on the spot. She accepted, then she asked what exactly she was going to do.

"I don't know," I said. "But we'll figure it out."

At first, Juicy just came and sat in the room. Then I had her answering the phones. But Juicy had that great laugh, and it turned out that she was one of Gary's biggest fans. So we started having her sit with us on the air, and the rapport was just on fire. That's when the morning show really took off, when I had Gary and Juicy on my team. Juicy is now a bona fide star. She's on *Little Women: Atlanta* and is going to do a movie with Kevin Hart. She's just blown up. And it couldn't have happened to a sweeter lady.

Not long after I'd moved to Dallas, Alfred Liggins promised that if I succeeded in beating the number one station in our genre, he would syndicate me. When we got to number one, true to his word, Alfred got me on a station in St. Louis. Soon the show premiered on stations in Augusta, Georgia; Oklahoma City; and Alexandria, Louisiana. So I was on the radio in five cities, and the tide just kept on rising.

———————

WHEN YOU FIRST get in the comedy business, everybody wants to be the next Eddie Murphy.

You want to be a movie star. You can imagine your picture on the cover of *Time* magazine. You want to be able to write your own ticket, whether it's having a live special on HBO, producing a movie that features your heroes like *Harlem Nights*, or getting an offer to host the Academy Awards.

When you first start out, you're reaching for the sky. And then you get to a point where you think, "I don't know if I like it up here; let me go back down to this level, where I'm not as high but I can breathe more easily."

You have to figure out your own truth. You have to make your own choices.

One of my first big choices, though I didn't see it as anything significant at the time, was my decision not to use blue language up onstage. I'm not putting down comedians who curse. But when I started performing at open mic night at the Comedy Club, we weren't allowed to swear. So I learned early on that I could be funny without that.

I'm not saying that I'm perfect. I say a few bad words from time to time. And I've made my share of jokes that I later reconsidered, thinking I was maybe too harsh and should have gone in another direction. But generally, I try to keep my humor clean. Cursing is just not part of my flow.

I also realized pretty quickly that if you're busy running after the Joneses, you could follow them right over a cliff. And I definitely didn't want to follow the Joneses to Los Angeles.

I had plenty of people in my ear telling me I needed to pack my bags and head to Southern California. "Oh, man, if you were here, your career would really blow up. You could be the next Kevin Hart!"

So in the beginning, I went on auditions. Lots of auditions.

"Cool beans!" the casting agent would say, grinning and nodding her head. Then, behind my back, she'd mumble, "We're not going to use him."

Then I did a showcase at the world-famous Comedy Store.

"We love you! You're great! Cool beans!" all the agents said. I couldn't get to the men's room for all the agents singing my praises.

Then I didn't hear a peep from any of them.

It was disappointing, at first. And then I realized what would be even more disappointing—all of those agents calling me back and booking up my schedule, and my having to move to LA.

Do you know how long it takes to shoot a film? You make all that money, but you can't enjoy it, because you are so busy chasing a role in the next movie, and the next, and the next.

I don't want somebody telling me "cool beans" when they don't mean it. Don't give me the runaround. My ego is not that fragile. That's why I'm not in LA, and that's why I'm not trying to be what I call "famous famous."

What I mean by that is, I'm not going for mega-movie-star, Oscar-winning famous. I'm not saying that with any regrets. I have a great career, and I'm doubly blessed, because I have balance. I can go do a movie or a comedy show in Los Angeles or New York, and then I can come home to something quiet.

I can go to Dreamland in Tuscaloosa or Birmingham, sit at the bar, and eat a quarter slab of ribs and not be bothered. Some of the customers may recognize me, but it's not overwhelming or intrusive. That's peace to me, just being able to walk in, have people treat me nicely, eat some great food, and then walk out without worrying. I don't need some paparazzi or bloggers ready to tell the world that I spilled barbecue sauce on my shirt.

I'm genuinely happy to see the mega-success enjoyed by people like Kevin Hart, whom I truly love and respect. He is unbelievably talented and yet so humble. He's been a friend to *The Rickey Smiley Morning Show*, always dropping by and spending time with us. He is a wonderful brother, and I'm proud of all that he has done.

But success has also taken a heavy toll on some of the greatest entertainers the world has ever seen. Prince: dead. Whitney Houston: dead. Michael Jackson: dead. You hear Whitney singing with the Georgia Mass Choir, her angelic voice soaring above all the rest. You see the genius of Prince and Michael, electrifying the stage. And they barely touched middle age.

When each of them died, that was just so personal to me. It hurt me so bad. To have grown up enjoying their gifts, and to see them pass so young, and so tragically, was hard to accept.

Too much of anything isn't good for anybody. And when you get to the point where you can't be a normal person, when you can't find a place in the world where you can just be yourself—when you may not even know sometimes who your self *is*—that's a serious problem.

A lot of people take drugs or drink heavily to cope. But I can stand here and say that I've never had a mixed drink or a joint in my life. I barely drink wine. The strongest stimulant I ever have in my system is a cup of coffee.

I haven't "crossed over" to the point where a large white audience knows who I am, and there are plenty of black people who don't recognize me. And I'm okay with that. I am famous enough.

I can go to church and not be bothered. I can get off the air at ten in the morning and go jump on the trampoline. Or I can go down by the lake, cast a fishing rod into the water, and just enjoy the quiet and presence of God, with the wind blowing and the trees swaying.

I can go to the cemetery to clean off my grandmothers' graves when I want, and ride through the streets of Birmingham with the doors off my Jeep, blasting Fleetwood Mac. That's peace and balance, and it's worth millions to me.

And God is so good. God has it just right. Most of the time, radio doesn't even feel like a job to me, because I love what I do. I'm able to use this platform, on the air in eighty cities, to help others. It's helped me fuel the Rickey Smiley Foundation, giving cars, cash, and support to hundreds of my listeners and others who are in need.

"Thank you for the praise," my listeners tell me. "Thank you for that doctor you had on. His advice helped me. Thank you for introducing me to that activist. I'd never heard of him, but he made me think."

Of course, life is definitely more complicated now. I may not be the biggest star in the world, but there's still a much bigger burden on my shoulders. I have a brand to uphold. I have employees depending on me. If a market drops me, if I lose my show, they lose their jobs. That's a lot of responsibility.

And sometimes, I think about how happy I was when all my success was just a dream. When Brandon was seven, I lived in a simple town house. He'd come over every other weekend, and he would ride his go-kart, or we'd cook waffles and watch the sun rise. We were happy.

I've tried to hold on to some of that simplicity. I travel to comedy clubs, stretching from Dallas to Charlotte to Miami, on the weekends. I do my radio show during the week. Then, many weekday mornings, as soon as I'm off the air, I'm heading to my grandfather's house.

"Go up there and get you a sandwich, and make me one, too," he says when I walk in the front door. "Then come on back and lay down, because I know you're tired."

Then, with the sandwiches and gingersnaps flowing, we watch *The Price Is Right* or Maury Povich or *Judge Judy*. See, you have to have peace and balance, balance and peace.

You can't let people tell you what you need to do. Sometimes they may have good intentions, and sometimes they may be just blowing smoke, but you have to be thoughtful and figure out what's best for you.

I have some friends who grew up in the projects with me. They're not working in particularly high-profile jobs, and they may not make as much money as I earn, but instead of resenting my success, they are out-of-their-minds proud of me. Half a dozen of them, along with their wives, will buy tickets and come see me perform at Jazz in the Gardens in Miami, or an arena in Jackson, Mississippi, forever showing their love and support.

You're rich when you have friends who revel in your success, and when your grandparents and teachers and coaches have given you enough wisdom that you can reflect on it for days at a time, and the well never runs dry.

You're blessed when you have a superstar like Eddie Murphy treating you like a brother in his home, and a childhood friend like Corey, who will make the introduction that sets you on your way.

You're lucky when people like Pierre and Earthquake, who are chasing the same dream, will let you bunk at their homes for free and, when you steal the show, lift you off your feet to celebrate.

I may not be "famous famous"—but I'm good.

HANDLE YOUR BUSINESS

I have issues with a lot of new ways of communicating. People collect folks on Facebook and act like all of those anonymous people are their true friends. Some of us get so busy taking pictures to post on Instagram that we miss out on actual moments—an awesome sunset, our son's winning touchdown—that truly make life special.

But there is one new way to stay in contact with people that I love, and that's texting, because texting gives you space. Space is critical. You need to have enough of it so that you can think, so that you aren't impulsive, and so that you aren't rushed into making a bad decision.

When LeBron James or Steph Curry is on the court, he doesn't aim for the basket while another player is blocking him nose to nose. He steps back, gets some perspective, and then takes his shot. To focus, to score those points, he needs to carve out some space.

That's why I don't answer my phone. As a matter of fact, for the past few years, I've kept my phone on silent at all times because I want people to text me. That includes my own kids, especially my oldest son, Brandon. He's good for calling at the drop of a hat and insisting that whatever he's asking for has to be done right then. Texting allows me time to think about how I want to respond. And I'm telling you, not being available to others whenever they feel like ringing you up can save you a lot of headaches, a lot of stress, and a lot of grief.

Texting allows you to control the conversation. If you pick up the phone after you've been working all day, and you just want to take a hot shower, you might get caught by your cousin Ruby. She gets you all distracted, telling you about the family reunion coming up in two months, how she just broke a fingernail, and oh, by the way, can she borrow $40?

Now, since you've wanted to get off the phone since you first picked up the receiver, you say yes just to get rid of her. But that $40 you just gave away was money you needed to pay for your daughter's field trip or your train fare so you could get to work the rest of the week. A phone call can pressure you into a situation that you don't need to be involved with. I had to learn that the hard way.

I'm a naturally generous person. I bought neighborhood kids toys and food when I was barely making any money, and so when I got successful, I wanted to help everybody. If you were looking for a job, I would buy you a used car so that you could get around more easily. If you were heading to college, I'd gladly pay for your books.

But I began to realize that people were trying to take advantage of me, like I had "ATM" stamped on my forehead. And worse, they were becoming dependent. If they got a flat tire, they had to call Rickey. If they really wanted to buy tickets to see Drake in concert, they had to call Rickey. If there was a new set of Adidas they really wanted, they came looking for Rickey.

I realized that I had to put a stop to all of that, whether the requests were flowing from family members, friends, or casual acquaintances. Now, that's not to say that I don't give. I do give a lot. But I set limits and conditions.

I may still buy you those schoolbooks, but I want to see your report card at the end of the semester. I may still pay to fix that flat tire, but only if you prove to me you have no other way to get to your job.

I will give you seeds to plant your own corn, but I'm not going to just give you the corn that I worked hard to grow. I'll give you a fishing pole and maybe even the bait, but you're not going to sit up in my kitchen, with your plate, knife, and fork, waiting for me to deliver the bass that I got up early in the morning to go catch.

I know a lot of good-hearted people who want to do all they can to help their relatives or friends, especially if they're the one in the group who's got a decent job and maybe a little money in the bank. But beyond the basics that you should provide to your own children, and maybe your parents, you don't owe anybody anything.

You have to be no-nonsense, so that you don't get used. If you don't set boundaries, you might wind up broke *and* bitter. You give everybody everything they ask for, and then in the end, everybody has something except you, and then you can't even get those same people to buy you a loaf of bread.

My wise and observant grandmother Mattie used to talk to me about that, especially when I started making money. Before she passed away, she warned me to put something aside for myself. "All these people you've given money to haven't even bought you so much as a Krispy Kreme doughnut," she said. "All these people want to borrow your car, but they never offer to get it washed, or even bring you back a cup of coffee when they drop it off."

Now I have everybody trained not to ask me for a damn thing. And if they do, they've got to put it in writing, in a text, so that I can review the message, look at it again an hour later, and then look at it again the next day, and the next. Unless you're on the way to the hospital, your urgent need is not my emergency. I don't have to drop everything and reach for my wallet just because you dented your bumper or are worried that the tickets to see Nicki Minaj might sell out.

I have a right to read that text message eight, nine, or ten times before I reply. Then, if I decide I want to help the person messaging me, I can take some space and time to negotiate the terms.

Some people think negotiations are only necessary in business, that discussions or deals are only something for movie stars, musicians, or moguls on Wall Street to engage in. But I don't care if you're working at a pizza parlor, babysitting your neighbor's kid, or driving a truck, you always need to be willing to speak up for what is best for you.

I meet people all the time who are mad about what they get paid, and I ask them, what did they negotiate when they agreed to take the job? Even if they can't change the salary, maybe they can discuss the hours that work best for their schedule or set a speedier timetable for when they can revisit the discussion about their pay, if they perform well.

And negotiating is not just something you should do when you're getting hired for a new job. Life is a negotiation. You don't have to give people everything they ask for. If a friend or relative calls you up asking for one hundred dollars, why can't you give them thirty dollars instead? Let them figure out some other people that they can go to for the rest of what they say they need.

Or maybe you do give them the full amount, but you set conditions. Let your cousin Darryl know that you want the money paid back in a certain amount of time, or if you want to make it a gift, tell him that once you give him that $100 bill, he can't ever come back to you to borrow another dime.

I talk to my listeners about matters like these all the time. You have to handle your business. I know that some of them worry that if they refuse to give a handout, their friends or relatives will get angry. And often, that will be the case. People are good at making others feel guilty, especially if they see the person they want to borrow from as successful. I'm not just talking about people who become wealthy superstars. You can be a manager at Kroger's or a supervisor at a construction site, and you might have people whispering behind your back that "you've changed" or cursing you out at the family reunion, because you don't grant them every favor that they request.

But why should you? Why should others be entitled to the fruits of your labor when you're the one who spent hours studying in school, or you're the one who drives an hour in the dark to work the late shift?

It's like watching a swan gliding across a pond. The crows may envy the swan's graceful, seemingly effortless movement, but the crow doesn't see that swan's feet frantically paddling beneath the surface, or the insects nipping at its belly. People don't know what you went through to get what you got, and unfortunately, many do not care.

I tell my listeners who call in to my radio show that, no, you don't have to cosign a loan to get your niece a car. No, you don't have to chip in for the down payment on your brother's house. And no, you don't have to work all day at the post office, driving Uber, or running your business, and then come home and answer a thousand phone calls, when all you want to do is watch television or take a nap.

If you're a schoolteacher who's been up since dawn, or a courier for the United Parcel Service who's been delivering boxes all day, why can't you take a couple of hours in the evening for yourself? Why do you have to call somebody back as soon as you get off work? Why can't they wait?

If a person wanting to borrow money can't understand the boundaries you set, you might have to consider cutting them off. There are people who will watch you work hard, but they'll never offer to treat you to a massage or even bring you lunch. That's why you have to be strong and be prepared to let some people go, even if it's your aunt or your cousin. They might think you owe them half of every paycheck because you once ate a bowl of cereal at their house. You can't get bogged down worrying about people who wouldn't do for you what they ask of you.

I have had to cut off plenty of people in my life, people whom I tried to help and build up. I remember that I once hired a guy to work behind the scenes on my radio show. He was a member of my fraternity, and in the spirit of brotherhood, I really wanted to help him out. He lived in Nashville, so I paid for his move to Birmingham. I even bought him a tailor-made suit, so that he would be sharp on his first day at work.

He didn't appreciate a thing. First of all, he was disrespectful, asking the women in the office to run errands for him, like he was their boss, and just being arrogant and rude. Even when, instead of firing him, I found him a new position working with another fraternity brother—Steve Harvey of all people—he had the nerve to *still* talk about me like I was a dog.

I won't lie. It was disappointing to extend myself so much, and to receive such disrespect in return. But over the years, I've worked out a way to deal with that type of situation. For people who show that kind of ingratitude, I turn around and bury them. Not in the way that you might think. I have a funeral for them in my head.

You might want to try it. In my mind, I read the obituary. I recite parts of the Old and New Testaments. I sing "Precious Lord, Take My Hand," and then I go and actually get myself something to eat and have a funereal repast.

I don't do all that for everybody, but know this: once you get me to that point, we are truly done. If we ever cross paths again, the best you might get from me is a head nod, and that's if I acknowledge you at all. You just have to leave some people behind. It may be painful at first, but I promise you that when you shut the door on those people who want to take advantage of you, or don't appreciate all that you've already done, God will give you a whole new set of true and loyal friends. He just needs you to create space, so that he can usher them into your life.

―――――――――――

OF COURSE, NOT everybody is out to get you. Some people may truly need help or guidance. But you cannot fix everyone else's problems. Most of us have plenty of our own troubles piled high on our plates. And unless you've been to seminary or medical school, you're probably not trained to help everyone with the serious trials they may be going through.

I'm not saying you should be dismissive of other people's suffering. You can be a good listener, if you have the time. You can offer your condolences or make a recommendation about where someone can get the help that they need. But we also have to protect our own mental health, our own space, so that we don't break down and become unable to handle all of our own responsibilities.

I actually keep a list of counselors, spiritual leaders, social workers, and ministers, so that I can refer people to professionals when they are troubled. I will suggest that an acquaintance speak to his or her pastor, or that a fan check out a ministry that has helped me in the past.

I do that because I want people who are struggling to get the solace they need. But I also don't want all of their burdens to fall on me. You've got to be conscious of the energy that you let into your own space, the thoughts that you let into your head. When you spend all day listening to how your next-door neighbor's leg is swelling up, and how bad Parkinson's disease is getting for your brother's father-in-law, by the time you get into bed, you can't even rest, because you feel so heavy. And you've got to rest, because you have your own problems to solve.

And that brings me to one of my favorite words in the English language: "no."

"No" is a complete sentence that requires no explanation. And I make no apologies for saying it to strangers whom I just met or even people who are a big part of my life.

People often get angry when you tell them no, which is puzzling to me. If you ask a favor, isn't "no" a potential answer? Why get mad when that's what you hear?

I look people in the eye and say "no" with no apologies. If they have a decent attitude, I may tell them my reasons why. Either way, everyone needs to know how to say that word with confidence and power. People may hate to hear it, but they'll get over it. And the word "no" will save you a lot of headaches in the meantime.

I don't just say "no" to people asking something of me. I say "no" to people trying to do a favor for me, as well.

I learned that lesson a long time ago, from the sales manager at 95.7 in Tuscaloosa. His name was Tim McReynolds. He was a tall, sophisticated, caramel-complexioned man, whom I'd find several times a day standing outside the station's doors, puffing on a cigarette. When I got off the air, preparing for the long drive home to Birmingham, I'd stop to stand outside with him and just absorb his knowledge. He's dead and gone now, but he gave me some of the best advice that I've ever gotten.

"Don't ever take anything for free, Rickey," he would say. "You've got a job. You're doing well. Pay for everything yourself. Because when people give you stuff, they hold it over your head, and they'll act like you owe them for the rest of your life."

I don't let people wave me into a club. I've got $20 to pay at the door. I won't accept a discount when I go to a restaurant for dinner. I let people know that I want to be charged the full price. I don't need to be given a table when a dozen other people are waiting. I'm no better than anybody else, so I'm fine waiting my turn in the crowd. And I'll let a restaurant manager know that if they want to hook somebody up, they should take care of the single mother who can barely afford to be eating there. Let her cut the line and feel special for an evening.

If a restaurant insists on not charging me, I'll leave the full amount of my bill in the form of a tip. This is because I know the waiter or waitress could use it, but also because I don't want to be on the hook the next time I see the restaurant's owner. I don't want to be on the hook *every* time I see the restaurant's owner.

No, I don't have a pair of concert tickets to give you because you gave me a free breakfast. No, you can't come sit in on my show when I'm interviewing Mary J. Blige. No. No. No. Did I stutter?

Both of my grandmothers used to say, "Kill it before it grows," which basically means don't start something that you can't finish. And man, I had to take that to heart in so many ways, the more famous I became. Now I even have to set boundaries with my fans.

Early on, everything was fine. People would ask for an autograph or somebody might want to snap a picture with their camera, and I was more than happy to oblige. But then social media came on the scene. Everybody had a cell phone, and everyone wanted a selfie, so that they could post a shot on Facebook.

I had to get organized. Often, I don't take photographs at all, but if

I do, I tell my team to line people up, take the person's cell phone to snap a picture, and then immediately escort them out. If you don't do that, folks linger, conversations start, requests are made, and you can never move on to the next person—or ever get home.

I learned that assembly-line approach from former president and first lady Barack and Michelle Obama. When you'd visit the White House and snap a picture with them, as soon as you'd blink your eyes and open them again, you'd be in the next room. They'd move your behind out of there so fast, it made your head spin, to the point where you wondered if you'd really stood there and met them at all.

It took a couple of years for me to get the routine down, but I had no choice. If people could hang out longer than it took to shake my hand, I'd be under siege. Everybody who made T-shirts would have one for me and would want me to put it on. Everybody who owned a car dealership would want me to come by so they could put my picture on the wall. Everybody who'd ever written a book about how they used to be on crack and now they weren't on crack would want me to take a look and maybe help them find a publisher.

I must have nineteen portraits people have painted of me. They'd bring them backstage, and then all through the airport, I'd be carrying these pictures that were as big as a windshield, trying to get them home.

Some folks were just trying to be nice, showing me that they really appreciated me. But others were opportunists, and I had to keep all of these different agendas and motives in check. If I took a compact disc or even a business card from some folks, they would act like that dude at the club who suddenly seems to think that because he bought a lady a drink, he's her boyfriend and needs to be by her side all night.

If I ran into that person again, they'd want to know what I thought about their play, how I liked their CD, or what I thought of their book.

And then I'd have to explain that I hadn't had the time to listen to it or read it, or worse, I did, and I could not stand it.

So I simply say no—to the paintings, the compact discs, the business cards, and the books. I think honesty, with courtesy, is always the way to go. It's business, never personal.

———————

THE TEMPTATIONS WERE one of the greatest musical groups of all time. They recorded for Motown, which everyone knows was based in Detroit. But many of their artists had roots in Alabama, like Eddie Kendricks, who came from Birmingham and serenaded the world with his soulful falsetto.

I've actually modeled my style after Eddie, who was tall, thin, and had a goatee, like me. Before I go out onstage, I play the Temptations classic "Get Ready" to ramp up my energy, and I bound onto that stage like I'm preparing to run a forty-yard dash.

Eddie and his fellow Temptations were consummate showmen—tailored, talented, and always on top of their game. Those are the qualities that I believe you have to bring to whatever you do. I don't care if you mop floors or screw in lightbulbs for a living, you need always to operate in a spirit of excellence.

Even when your boss doesn't seem to appreciate you, even when a rude customer curses you out, try to keep your composure and a good attitude, because you never know who is watching. There might be someone else walking through the store, waiting at the Department of Motor Vehicles, or just watching you from a doorway who respects how you handle yourself. They might be sizing you up for another opportunity that could transform your life.

Even if that observer doesn't have some big job or business investment to hand you, they might give you that tip that allows you to buy something you need or make a sale that helps you meet your goal for the month.

I remember when I used to sell shoes at Foot Locker. I'd pull out twenty or thirty pairs, running from the storeroom downstairs back to the main floor, only to have the customer walk out that door without buying even a pair of socks.

But I couldn't treat the next customer with a bad attitude, just because the last customer disappointed me. And I couldn't ignore the woman with the shabby coat in order to focus all my attention and courtesy on the customer decked out in Louis Vuitton. On more than one occasion, it would be that modestly dressed person, who came in the store after a dozen others had walked out without buying a thing, who bought five or six pairs of shoes from me, making my day.

And even if the payoff isn't immediate, even if no one is watching you, you should still conduct yourself as a professional. When you carry yourself with dignity, you feel positive and proud.

I have a studio in my home. I could roll out of bed, sit down in that chair, and do my show in my pajamas, because no one would ever know. But I don't. I brush my teeth and get dressed every morning before I go on the air, because it makes me feel good. It makes me feel ready. I also do it because I appreciate every single one of my listeners. The least I can do is dress the part, even if I never walk out my front door.

WE ALL HAVE challenges. You might be worrying about a misbehaving child. You might have a health problem that you're trying to get over or a long-ago school debt that you're still trying to pay off. But you have to keep on handling your business anyway. Whatever your profession, the show must go on.

In 2000, I was in New York City to tape *106 & Park*, BET's popular show that counted down the top music videos. I was going to talk with the hosts, A. J. and Free, about the new season of *Comic View*, which I was going to be helming. I was just about to go onstage when my phone rang. The caller ID said it was my grandmother Mattie.

When I answered, it wasn't my grandmother on the line. It was Mrs. Lockhart, my grandmother's dear friend and neighbor, who lived across the street from her. Why was she calling me from my grandmother's house?

"Hi, Rick," she said. "Where are you?"

I told her that I was in New York. Then came the news.

"The paramedics had to come this morning for your grandmother," she said. "She didn't make it."

My son Brandon was sitting in the audience. The actress Vivica Fox had just gone onstage to talk about a project that she was involved in. And there I was, with my world collapsing around me.

But I had to block it out of my head. I had to go out there, with A. J. and Free, and do what I'd come to do.

"Rick," Mrs. Lockhart said, "are you all right?"

"Yes, ma'am," I lied. "I'm fine."

I hung up just when A. J. said, "Ladies and gentlemen, Rickey Smiley!"

I ran onstage smiling, did a short interview, and then took a couple of pictures. A few minutes later, I was grabbing Brandon, racing back to the hotel for our bags, and flying home to Birmingham.

As hard as it was to go out there on that stage, I knew it was what Mattie would have expected me to do. When her mother had died a couple of years earlier, I had an opportunity to open up for Bernie Mac and D. L. Hughley at the Township Auditorium in Columbia, South Carolina. I wasn't going to go. But even in the midst of her grief, Grandmother Mattie was her usual no-nonsense self.

"If I catch you in that church, you're going to have a problem," she said. "Mama is gone. You've already been to the funeral home. You don't need to be at the service. You go do that show."

I had to handle my business. The show had to go on.

A year later, when my grandmother Ada passed away, I was scheduled to perform in Pensacola, Florida, where I was going to be the headliner. I didn't want to crack jokes when my heart was broken, but I remembered Mattie's words. So I accompanied her and the rest of our family to the church for the service. We rode together in the procession to the cemetery for the burial, and then I went and did my show, in the same suit I'd worn to bury my beloved Ada.

But I was glad that I hadn't canceled my show, because some of the people in the audience that night might have lost someone they'd loved, too. Somebody might have just found out that they had cancer and needed to laugh. Somebody might have been looking forward to that show all week, to give them a few moments when they didn't have to focus on their own pain.

At least I'd been blessed to have known both of my grandmothers, who'd lived long, wonderful lives. I know I have fans who have had to endure so much. I had to smile for somebody else who might have lost much more than me.

For entertainers—singers, dancers, comedians—it's not all glamour and glory. Sometimes we have to make personal sacrifices to stand on a set or a stage and do what we do. And for me, it's not just about making money. It's also a ministry.

There are plenty of mornings when I wake up and I'm not really in the mood to be happy and telling jokes on the radio. Maybe I'm sad about a situation going on with my son Brandon, or I'm feeling discouraged because someone I helped along the way turned around and took me to court.

But then I remember that one of my listeners might have just gotten a deadly diagnosis. Maybe they just lost a spouse. I need to get on the air and offer them a word of inspiration. I need to play a song that might lift their mood.

I can walk onstage, look out in the audience, and see the despair in some of the people's eyes. I can tell when they have cancer or when they're withering away from AIDS. I can see when people are hurting.

I notice the man on the side sitting in a wheelchair, and I go out of my way to smile and make eye contact with him. When I'm shaking hands after I've performed, and I meet the woman with the chipped nails and the threadbare clothes, I hold her hands for a few seconds longer, because I know it took a lot for her to come to my show. I ask her how she is doing. I ask her if she enjoyed herself. I might even invite her backstage and take a few pictures.

I can feel the despair, and 99 percent of the time I have it right. Often, that person's friend will come to me afterward and say, "Thank you for doing that. You have no idea what they've been through."

Once, in Beaumont, Texas, I asked a woman to come backstage. I found out from one of her friends who came with her that she had stage-four breast cancer, and she was about to enter hospice care. I took pictures with that woman and gave her a compact disc with some of my prank calls. Not long after, that same friend mailed me her obituary and thanked me for what I had done. But I was the one who felt thankful. I felt thankful that God had blessed me with a profession and a platform that allowed me to bring a tiny bit of joy into so many wonderful people's lives.

Whatever you do, wherever you work, sometimes you have to go the extra mile. "Extra" is the key part of the word "extraordinary." Sometimes you do a little bit more than you feel like doing, you give a little more of yourself than you feel like giving, and you will reap the blessings. Even if another person doesn't notice, I can promise you that God will.

————

A KEY PART of growing, prospering, and succeeding is knowing how to listen. Sometimes, we get so defensive, so stuck in our old ways, that we take offense when someone tries to talk to us. But if you open your ears and heart, wisdom can come to you from unexpected places.

Gary with da Tea is a key part of my radio show crew and a star on my docuseries *Rickey Smiley for Real*.

Gary is over-the-top, dramatic, and funny on my shows. But Gary is one of the wisest, most business-savvy professionals that I have ever met. When I moved to Dallas from Birmingham, not only did he help me with the basics, like finding an apartment, but he also let me know that I had to up my game.

I was driving my Chevrolet Tahoe SUV and wearing my Nike sweat suits, and I felt like I was styling. After all, that's what I'd driven and worn in Birmingham, so I didn't question that they should be good enough in Dallas.

But in Birmingham, I was a local guy who'd done well. In Birmingham, I'd been a comedian for a couple of years on Doug Banks's show.

Now, in Dallas, I would be hosting my own program. Gary let me know that I couldn't move to Dallas with a Birmingham mind-set.

He was blunt, like an older, wiser brother. He told me that I had to grow. I needed to trade in that Tahoe for a new car. And like Steve Harvey said back when I introduced him at the Comedy Club, Gary told me that I needed to start dressing better. It was all well and good to stay humble on the inside, he said. But I was now a public figure, a star, with a show in one of the nation's biggest markets, and I needed to look the part.

One morning, Gary actually drove me over to the parking lot behind a rival radio station, so I could get a look at the cars that the talent over there was driving. I got the message.

I hadn't seen myself as a personality in the same sense as Doug Banks or Steve Harvey. And I was caught up in the idea of staying true to my hometown.

I could have gotten an attitude with Gary, asking who he thought he was to tell me what to do. I could have gotten my back up or descended into arrogance. But I recognized that Gary had a tremendous amount of knowledge. He had been in the radio game for a long time, and he knew Dallas.

I recognized that Gary was probably one of the smartest people I'd ever met in my life. And so I was smart enough to listen.

I bought a new Range Rover. Gary also took me to a Neiman Marcus outlet, and I bought Ted Baker shirts, a few pairs of True Religion jeans, and some nice shoes that I'd put on whenever I made an appearance. I was looking casual but sophisticated, just in time for the rise of social media. And I saw the difference it made in my career. When you look successful, you draw more success. Truly, it works.

You don't have to spend a ton of money on fancy outfits or charge up your credit cards trying to look fly. But you need to always remember that you are your most important representative. Nobody can make the case for you better than you can. And so you want to present yourself well. You want to look the part.

Whatever you are trying to do, whether it's rising through the ranks at your job, operating and growing your business, or saving enough money to buy a home, it's important to listen. If your heart and ears are open, you're less likely to miss wisdom when it flows your way.

That's all just common sense, which always comes in handy as you build a career. Common sense and common courtesy can take you far.

When Alfred Liggins decided to give me a chance to host my own radio show, I thanked him for the opportunity. I send Cathy Hughes, Alfred's mother and the legendary founder of Radio One, flowers once a month. I want to show appreciation for the fact that her and her son's belief in me took my career to a whole other level.

Whether they're writing jokes or helping me decorate my home, I send flowers, a fruit basket from Edible Arrangements, or a thank-you card to anybody who does business with me. And why not? If you are doing a good job, helping me to do what I need, I want to show you that I respect that.

Even if relationships run their course, I keep it cordial. It's important never to spit on your way out the door. While you know where you've been, you don't know where you're going or who you might need one day. And even if you never cross paths with that person again, you likely gained something from that experience that can propel your future.

When I got fired from *The Doug Banks Morning Show*, I called

Doug and thanked him for the chance he'd given me. Doug wasn't responsible for my being let go. I wasn't clicking with the program manager at the station that carried the show in New York City.

But even if Doug had been the one to make that decision, I still would have offered him my appreciation. His show had given me another level of exposure and a chance to further polish my on-air persona. That was worth acknowledging. My getting fired was very minor compared to the days I was on the air with him and all the success in my life that came after.

I'd maintained the right attitude from day one. I took a role on that show with the determination to make Doug shine. I wanted to contribute to the on-air chemistry, not to overshadow it. I wanted the show to be great. I believe that God knows what your motives are. He knows if you're sincere and have integrity. I think that because I had the right disposition, both when I worked for Doug Banks and on my way out the door, God favored me. Within two or three years, I was right back in those same markets with *The Rickey Smiley Morning Show*.

At times, it's hard for me to understand former employees who've talked about me like I'd run them over with my Jeep because I didn't renew their contracts. They forgot or failed to acknowledge the 365 days we worked together, when they were able to feed their families because of the money I paid them. Not to mention the opportunity I gave them, even if our relationship eventually came to an end.

Whenever you leave, you need to leave right. Not all relationships work out. When I married my wife, Terri, I expected to stay married forever. But that didn't happen. When I worked for Doug Banks, I figured I'd be on his nationally syndicated show for years. But that didn't work out.

When a connection comes to an end, you've got to use what you learned from the journey and move forward with some humility. Hopefully, you have a little more knowledge than you had before. And remember that often, when God closes one door, it's to open another. What's waiting on the other side may be greater than anything you've ever imagined.

ON REDEMPTION

I loved growing up in the projects.

When I was about seven years old, my mother, sister, and I moved out of my grandmother's home and into Morton Simpson Village, which for some reason everybody called the Kingston Projects.

There were no bad days there. I always had a bunch of other kids to play with, and we lived within walking distance of our church. Everybody had flowers on their porches and their own piece of neatly mowed lawn stretching out in front.

We all put clay bunny rabbits in our windows for Easter, hung twinkling wreaths on our front doors for Christmas, and kept our lights on all night to celebrate Martin Luther King Jr.'s birthday. We took pride in our little pocket of Birmingham. I didn't know for the longest time that there was supposed to be a stigma attached to a housing project, or that in the minds of many people, the projects were associated with anguish and crime. Every once in a while, somebody's hubcaps got stolen, or a couple of knuckleheads got in a fight, but that was about as bad as it ever got. There really wasn't any suffering in Kingston, only joy.

I remember waking before the sun came up and standing at the window, watching the giant yellow trucks scoop up all the trash, then dump those mountains of paper and aluminum into a bin. The lights would be flashing, and a whirl of noise would rattle my neighbors from their sleep.

Beep beep! Whirrrrr.

I'd stand there, my eyes wide and my heart beating fast. "Man," I would think. "I want to drive a truck and dump a bin just like that one day." It was an everyday chore, but it was exciting to me.

I'd lost my father, whom I barely knew, when I was just a little boy, but I didn't feel lingering sadness. That is, until we moved away from the projects, to a complex that was supposed to be a step up but was really a step down into misery.

I was in high school by then, and days would sometimes pass without my mother coming home. I remember walking the few blocks from the cluster of apartment buildings where we lived to my grandmother's apartment. I'd sit on her porch gazing out into the street, and I would see a figure dart by. Was that my mom?

Before I could get up and put on my shoes, she would be gone, having disappeared down a side street, around a crowded corner, into a cloud of smoke—from a crack pipe.

That was when I knew my life had hit bottom.

YOU CAN'T DEFINE people by their worst behavior, just like you cannot reduce life to its lowest moment. We would never be able to celebrate if we dwelled only on the negative. We'd never have a happy day if we chose to just wallow in regret.

And just like it's important for each and every one of us to forgive others, so that we are not poisoned by our own rage, we also have the right to ask for forgiveness when we do wrong. For that lie we told when we were afraid, that punch we threw when we weren't thinking straight, that mistake we made when we were young or misguided and simply didn't know any better. When we try to make amends, or simply have enough humility to apologize, each of us is worthy of redemption.

There may be some things that are a bridge too far, some acts that are so heinous or evil that forgiveness or redemption just can't happen. But for most of the transgressions that folks commit on any given day, the misspeaking and the misstepping, I think people deserve a second chance.

My mother, Carolita, has always been a sweet soul. She had a half sister, Kathy, but growing up, my mother was the only girl in a house full of tough, protective brothers. She experienced heartbreak when she was young, first losing my father to the streets, and then losing him for good when he was killed far away from her in New York City. But she was resilient. And she had a whole network of parents, grandparents, siblings, and friends to help care for me and my younger sister.

She could be a disciplinarian when she needed to be, but she was also one of those young parents who was full of fun. I remember that she used to take me to concerts. When I was just five or six years old, I saw Bootsy Collins, with his sky-high boots and star-shaped shades. I was there in person when the Ohio Players sang about skintight britches and Leroy "Sugarfoot" Bonner crooned "Sweet Sticky Thing."

I even went with my mother and her sister-in-law, my aunt Betty, to see the sex symbol Teddy Pendergrass. When he sang "Turn Off the Lights," he turned off Aunt Betty's lights for real, because she passed out. Teddy had that effect on women.

And one of my brightest memories is sitting at the edge of the stage when George Clinton and the Mothership touched down. There wasn't a Parliament-Funkadelic lyric that I didn't know and couldn't sing in my sleep.

When my mother, her friends, and I would step out to a show, we would be dressed to the nines—I'm talking crinkly leather jackets, platform shoes, and smooth silk shirts. One time, when I was eight years old, we went to a concert at the Boutwell Memorial Auditorium in Birmingham. Kool and the Gang was tearing the roof off with their hit "Jungle Boogie," and the last act of the night was the one and only James Brown.

During the final intermission, before James Brown took the stage, there was a contest to determine who was the best-dressed person in Boutwell. I had on a white suit with a white bow tie, white shoes, white socks, and a purple silk shirt. I was so sharp that my mother encouraged me to go up onstage and vie for the prize.

I walked to the stage, and the emcee pulled me out in front of what must have been five thousand people. I'd never stood in front of a crowd that huge, and when they saw me, folks started screaming like crazy.

I was competing against another little boy who was probably my age or a year younger, also decked out in a snow-white suit. He and I made it to the final four contestants. Then it was down to just the two of us. It was hard to make out who the audience liked more, because each of us got deafening applause. Finally, the emcee declared a tie and said he was going to give each of us $100.

A hundred dollars? The most I ever had in my pocket was the five or six dollars my grandfather Ernest would give me after I helped him mow some lawns. "Mama," I wanted to yell out, "we're rich!"

The other little boy and I were escorted backstage, and we got to shake James Brown's hand. It was the first time I'd ever met a celebrity. And on top of that, I got handed a crisp $100 bill.

When we got that money, I looked at the other little boy, and he looked at me, and our smiles were so wide it's a wonder our cheeks didn't crack. We stuck our prize money in our pockets and walked back to our seats with our chests puffed out and the applause still ringing in our ears.

With my prize money, Mama got each of us a new dresser, and she bought me a big yellow Tonka truck.

My mother was always generous, especially at Christmas. Of course, I didn't initially realize how giving she actually was, because I thought Santa Claus was the one dropping off all of those presents spilling out from under our tree.

But when I was about eight, I started to get suspicious. We didn't have a chimney, so how did Santa get in?

That Christmas morning, I went upstairs and woke my mother up.

"Listen, let me ask you something," I said very seriously. "They say Santa comes down the chimney, but we don't have one. How does he bring us our presents?"

My mother had been partying the night before and had probably just gone to bed, since she had to outlast my sister and me to stuff the final gifts under the tree. But I swear she spun a story off the top of her head that was worthy of a Pulitzer Prize.

"Well," she said, "Santa has to go to the Housing Authority to get the master key. Then he parks the sleigh in the middle of the projects and goes from house to house while we are asleep."

Then she lay back down and rolled over.

"Hmm," I thought. "That makes sense. Kind of. But what's the Housing Authority?"

I was momentarily satisfied and walked back down the stairs. My mother, as usual, had laid out a fabulous Christmas. We always had a real tree nearly toppling over from all the candy canes, lights, and ornaments. The boxes were piled high, filled with dolls, toy cars, and enough clothes to fill two or three closets.

But something was missing. I'd asked for a football, and Santa hadn't brought it.

Back up the stairs I went.

"Santa forgot to bring my football," I said, shaking my mother awake.

My mother sat up, her hair smashed to one side. Then she reached under her bed, grabbed the forgotten football, and handed it to me.

"Here," she said. "Now, don't wake me up again."

I was happy to get my football. But I wasn't so sure that I believed in Santa Claus anymore.

———————

MAMA ALWAYS WORKED. I remember that for a while, she had a job at Arby's, and to this day I can't eat anything they serve. I got so tired of that food she used to bring home. She'd take a bunch of those little thin strips of beef and try to put them back together, like that made a real roast. It didn't. Once that meat is cut up, it should stay that way. But I'll give my mother points for trying.

Mama also used to sell a little weed on the side. My mother's a deacon now, very strong in her faith. But back then, she would actually take some of the little tithing envelopes from the church and use those to tuck the marijuana in. It wasn't right, but it *was* kind of inventive.

She wasn't some hard-core dealer. She and a lot of her friends smoked weed, so she was basically supplying her clique, and it was a way for her to earn some extra cash. Those additional dollars that she socked away are probably what enabled us to finally get to the point where we had enough money to move out of the Kingston Projects.

As much as I loved the projects, they really are supposed to be a stepping stone to something better. So when I was a teenager, we moved into a nearby apartment complex that didn't have a name but that everyone called the Bricks. I started going to Woodlawn High School, where I made a lot of friends, and I loved hanging out and going to the football games.

But times were changing. It was the 1980s, and people were starting to freebase cocaine. A drug epidemic began to infect a lot of families, and mine wasn't immune. My mother graduated from smoking weed to smoking crack.

I didn't know what was going on at first. I just knew that life had become strange. I'd never believed we were rich, but I'd never felt poor. Now, all of a sudden, money was tight. Previously, my mother had always had really cool friends whom I liked and felt comfortable around. Even when one of her buddies was so buzzed from smoking a blunt that he tripped, grabbed our Christmas tree to brace himself, and wound up sending it and all the ornaments crashing to the floor, the incident seemed silly and funny, not ominous or out of control.

But that particular friend, with his big cowboy hat, didn't come around anymore. Much of my mother's old crew had been replaced by people who I felt were shady. I didn't like them. And the few old friends who remained seemed different. My mother had some girlfriends who I'd thought were beautiful. They were the first crushes that I'd ever had. But now they were looking skinny and scruffy, like they weren't taking care of themselves. Something was wrong.

I never saw my mother smoke. She was still functional and always looked neat, with her jeans clean and her hair brushed back. But she stopped dressing up, or caring if my sister and I did. Her spark was gone. And then my grandmother Ada started dropping hints that my mother might be on drugs. That was devastating to hear, but it made sense.

I was embarrassed. Crack was everywhere, but it was a dirty word. Everyone knew that it was spurring people to violence and turning people who had been responsible, hardworking folks into desperate, yellow-eyed zombies.

I didn't know what to say or do. I wasn't going to confront my own mother and ask her if she was on drugs. So I had to block it out of my head and just pretend that it wasn't happening. Many children have to do that when their parents have a problem. It's the way that they cope.

I went off to college, and that made it easier to forget what might be going on at home. I would hang out on campus with friends. I pledged Omega Psi Phi and went to parties. But when I found myself between jobs and wrecked my car, I had to temporarily drop out of school. I went home to my grandmother Ada, who had actually moved out of her home and into the Kingston Projects. And then I discovered that crack cocaine had grabbed hold of my beloved projects, too. There didn't seem to be any escape.

I also had another problem weighing on my mind. My high school girlfriend had a baby that she now claimed was not mine. I felt like I'd been run over by one of those garbage trucks I used to watch from our apartment window.

In the midst of all that, I would sit on my grandmother's porch and see my mother flitting by. And I saw young guys out on the street, selling dope on the corner or leaning up against their cars. I was depressed. I was broke.

I could have stepped off of my grandmother's porch and started selling dope, too. It would have been a quick way to get some money in my pocket. Instead of repairing my wrecked car, I might have been able to buy a new one. I could have headed back to school with a sharp wardrobe and my tuition bill paid in full.

I had to make a decision. Should I stay on the porch or step off?

I decided to stay put. I only stepped off that porch to go to Sunday school and Sunday service. Those times at church became the only things that I looked forward to. I would sit up in church with tears in my eyes, not because I was sad, but because I was happy. Church provided a respite in my life. The choir's beautiful singing and all that worshipful praise reminded me of how good God was. For a few hours, joy would fill all the spaces inside me that felt empty. I sat in those pews and decided that I was going to stick with God, no matter what. I was going to stay on the porch.

I eventually started getting paid to play piano during Sunday school. And that money came in handy, because even though my girlfriend had told me that Brandon wasn't mine, I now had another child to raise. My fourteen-year-old sister was pregnant.

MY LITTLE SISTER, Karon, is five years younger than me, but we were always close. She'd get on my nerves like kid sisters do, annoying me and whining if I got one drop more of Kool-Aid than she did. But she was sweet, quiet, and smart. I remember that even as a teenager, she still had a baby face.

But Karon met an older guy, already out of high school, and I think she got manipulated. He had a nice car, and he probably filled her head with lots of talk about love and commitment that she was too young to even be thinking about. Karon was only in the ninth grade when my niece Porshé was born.

It looked a bit bleak at the time. My sister was a mother before she was anywhere near grown. I hate to admit it, but in the midst of our panic, there was talk about her having an abortion. But thankfully, we didn't have the money to carry that out. I won't even contemplate what life would have been like without our precious Porshé. She has been a blessing in so many ways, not the least of which is that she was the one who ultimately pulled my mother back from the edge.

You see, my mother was crazy about Porshé. She bathed her, bought her baby clothes, and sang to her at night. There wasn't anything she wouldn't do for that baby. But crack was still riding my mother like a demon.

One day, Mama sold some food stamps that were meant to buy milk and groceries to feed Porshé, so that she could cop some drugs.

That was my mother's breaking point.

I picked up a ringing phone, and it was Mama, crying on the line.

"I'm done," she said.

"Done with what?" I asked her.

"I'm done," is all she would say. "Come get me. I'm tired."

I had a car again, so I drove to the home of my aunt Nanny, my grandmother's aunt. When I pulled up, my mother was sitting on the hood of a truck, tears in her eyes.

"I want to get help," she said, telling me about the food stamps. She wanted to be healed. She wanted to be redeemed.

I asked around and heard about a place called Aletheia House that worked with addicts. We didn't have the money to pay for my mother to enter the inpatient program, but the people at Aletheia House were incredibly helpful and told us about an outpatient program that they also ran.

My mother took advantage of it, and since that day twenty-eight years ago, she has been drug- and alcohol-free.

Mama's life kept going up and up. She met and married my step-father, Edward Lester, and together they are deacons at Guiding Light Church, often leading the worship service. She is pushing seventy, and she has more fun now than she ever did, going out fishing as often as she can. And she is an awesome mother and grandmother.

Despite that rough period in both of our lives, I've never been angry with my mother. Even in the grip of her addiction, she still let me and my sister know that she loved us. But even if I had been mad, why would I stay in that dark place after my mother had turned her life around? She worked hard and got clean. She has made up for selling those food stamps a million times over, and I appreciate it.

———————

KARON AND HER boyfriend had a second daughter, my niece Kyrisha, whom we call ReeRee, also before she graduated high school.

But it's what happened when my sister got pregnant the first time, with Porshé, that still makes my blood run cold.

When the church mothers found out Karon was carrying a baby out of wedlock, they whispered about how shameful it was. And do you know what they and the church's old-fashioned pastor did? They made my sister stand up before the congregation and apologize for getting pregnant.

When I found out, I cursed so much that my grandmother had to keep me from racing straight to the church. I felt that if there was anybody in that sanctuary who had not sinned, let them throw the first stone. And believe me, I knew that there was no one in there who had the moral authority to lift a pebble.

How could they? How dare they? Only a few years after Porshé was born, I was there attending Karon's high school graduation. Both of her daughters were there, chattering and cooing in the background, and I was proud that, as hard as it was, my sister had gotten her diploma *and* she'd graduated in four years because she was *that* smart and *that* determined. She didn't have anything to apologize for.

Not long after Karon earned her diploma, my great-grandparents made her and the girls' father get married. It was like a shotgun wedding straight out of *The Color Purple*. They went to that same judg-mental pastor's house and exchanged vows. But the marriage didn't last long. That guy had gotten her pregnant twice, but he wasn't in-terested in being a father or a husband. So Karon ended up raising the girls on her own, with a lot of love and support from our entire family.

I've always been my sister's protector, and I basically became the girls' father as well. Anything they needed—hair bows, Easter dresses, Christmas toys—I made sure they had it. My sister never felt entitled to any of the trappings of my success. She never asks for a dime, but I have always tried to help her and the girls out as much as I can.

And those girls are awesome. I paid for Porshé's college education, and she is now a graduate of the famous, historically black Clark Col-lege in Atlanta. Not only did Porshé avoid having children at a young age, but she's also founded a celibacy support group and is immersed in her church.

Porshé was the first of all of my babies to graduate from college, and after she walked across that stage, I had to go someplace quiet and sit by myself to gather my emotions. She is a brilliant, hardworking young lady with a bachelor of arts degree. She lights up any room that she stands in and is a mentor to my oldest daughter, D'essence. This is the child that my sister once had to apologize for bringing into this world. I'd love to see the faces of those church mothers now.

And two summers ago, I walked ReeRee down the aisle. She's twenty-five years old, and she and the wonderful guy she married al-ready have their own business.

That wedding was amazing. Everyone in my family loves *Love & Hip Hop: Atlanta*, so I booked Momma Dee, one of the show's funni-est characters, to sing at the ceremony as a surprise. People cracked up, saying that only I would think to book Momma Dee to sing at a wedding. But everybody loved seeing her, and Momma Dee was simply awesome singing her single "In That Order."

Porshé and ReeRee's father was there as well, watching along with the other guests as I walked ReeRee down the aisle. After the ceremony, the girls' paternal grandfather said that he wanted to speak to me.

The room was crowded and loud, but when he was talking to me, looking me dead in the eye, it seemed like the music and chatter suddenly stopped. I could hear every word he said as clear as a bell.

He simply told me that I had done an excellent job caring for the girls, and that he appreciated it. He didn't exactly say it, but in that short, simple thank-you, I also heard an apology. An apology for what his son had done, getting involved with a young girl, and then what he had not done, since he shirked his responsibility by walking away from her and his children.

Those few words gave me closure, because I had avoided that side of my nieces' family pretty much all of their lives. When their grandfather shook my hand, he cleared the air of the resentment I'd felt toward his family, and even the anger I'd harbored toward his son. His granddaughter—my niece—had gotten some college under her belt, had built her own business, and was marrying the love of her life. By thanking me, I felt that he was saying he was sorry that he and his son hadn't been a bigger part of her journey and her sister's. And I was willing to accept his apology.

EACH OF US has a past, but we cannot let that obliterate our future.

Chris Brown, the talented pop star, is someone I have tried to mentor. He has had more than one run-in with the law. I was in Los Angeles in 2009, not long after he pleaded guilty to felony assault for hitting the superstar singer Rihanna, who had been his girlfriend at the time.

I saw Chris at the Sofitel hotel, where I was staying. I don't believe that you should ever hit a woman. But instead of piling on, I wanted to positively motivate Chris, to encourage him to get on and stay on a different path. I told him that you have to find people who bring out the best in you, not the worst. And if you feel the need to lash out, you have to show restraint and then move on. He took in those words of encouragement, and he gave me a big old hug.

If you don't give people a second chance, if you're not willing to let them make amends, then why would anyone ever try? Where would each of us be if we were only judged by the worst behavior we displayed?

I knew how to talk to Chris, because once I'd stood in his shoes. I knew what it was like to do something I deeply regretted and to have to make amends.

I'd met my wife, Terri, at a party when I was in college. She was beautiful and worked as a flight attendant. We dated for about a year, and when we finally decided to become husband and wife, we just drove to city hall and did it.

We were married for twelve years, and during that time, we had some serious arguments. One night, it got so bad that we started throwing things at each other. Then we started pushing each other and scratching. Finally, she called the police.

I was never a guy who would beat a woman, but I'd definitely had fights with girlfriends that had gone too far. They were silly situations, where one of us would be sitting in the car, and the other one would hop out and slam the door, and the two of us would keep on cursing each other out as the car rolled along at half a mile per hour.

But this tussle with Terri had gotten physical, and the cops took me to jail. I was performing by then, so I knew there was going to be negative publicity. But, truly, I was more concerned about what my grandparents would think, knowing what I had done and the fact that I was behind bars. I told myself that if I ever got out of that cell, I was never going to be in another one for as long as I lived.

I was quickly released, and part of the resolution to the charge was for me to attend a domestic violence prevention class. Instead of sulking or being resentful that I had to take a course, I appreciated the chance to avoid more jail time. And I wanted to take in the lessons the instructors were trying to teach us, so that I didn't end up in such a situation again.

They taught me what I tried to teach Chris, that you need to be around people who bring out the best in you. If you are around those who don't, you need to walk away. They emphasized that violence is never, ever the answer. Those words were a blessing to me, and I wanted to share them with Chris and anyone else who might need to hear them.

Another thing I learned from that episode in my life is that you cannot allow a mistake to define you. If the Lord gives you another day, another week, another year of life, take that opportunity to make amends, to do something positive, to reframe your image, for yourself as well as the world. Seek redemption, and then forgive yourself.

The way back from a mistake can be hard. When you've messed up, others might be slow to forgive. You might want to give up, convinced that your reputation will be stained forever. You don't think that doing better will make a difference, and that can lead to reverting to bad habits.

But that's why, when you're seeking redemption, the first person to ask for forgiveness is yourself. You have to believe that you deserve a second chance.

I was young, stupid, and caught in the heat of the moment when I fought with Terri all those years ago. That's not an excuse. What I did was wrong. But I have made amends. Today, Terri and I get along fine. And I have people coming up to me on the street, at the shopping mall, and at the airport, saying thank you for the Rickey Smiley Foundation, thank you for my words of encouragement on the radio, thank you for making them laugh at a moment when they were feeling low.

I didn't allow myself to be defined by a single bad situation. And since then, I've done way more good than bad. That's why I'm willing to talk about it, to share it with others, to let them know that I'm far from perfect, but I've been able to learn from my mistakes, to make up for them, and to move on.

Chris may still have a ways to go, but I think he has a good heart. After our talk, he came on my radio show, and he drew a picture for me. "Thanks for everything, Uncle Rickey," he wrote.

———————————

YOU KNOW HOW to come back from a mistake? You do good. You become successful and use the platforms that you have to inspire and help others.

Not everybody is going to forgive you. I'm sure some who read about what happened between me and Terri think I'm a bad dude. It may take years for you to right some of your wrongs, but you just make sure that when you tally it all up, the good outweighs the bad. And don't let people dangle your mistakes over your head like a sword. Bring up what you've done first, and then let them know what you've done since. Take away their power. Take away your shame.

Maybe you went to jail for shoplifting when you were a teenager. If someone throws that in your face, tell them, "Okay, I shoplifted. That was ten years ago. So what? Now I'm working at FedEx and going back to school, and all you want to talk about is how I stole some cookies from Walmart when I was eighteen?" Catch them off guard. Take away all their ammunition.

And don't just bring up your past to disarm others who want to judge you. Share your past with others who can learn from you. Remind a young person, or one of your troubled peers, that despite all the success you may be experiencing, you're not perfect. You've fallen down and bounced back, too.

Jay Z sold drugs when he was young. Sean "Puffy" Combs was the host of a basketball game that sparked a stampede that tragically turned deadly. But they grew. They rebounded. And now they are successful businessmen, fathers, and role models for a generation.

I do think that because we live in a time when social media is all around us, and people can throw stones, then hide behind anonymous profiles, it's gotten harder to move on from mistakes and the past.

I've seen it in the lives of my own children. One time, my son Malik said on our family's reality show that he sees black women as sisters rather than romantic interests. He happens to go to a school that is majority white, and he said that he just didn't find black girls attractive.

Malik is only fifteen, but you should have seen how grown folks went after him on social media. Instead of trying to change his way of thinking, initiating constructive conversations, they made my son—a teenage boy just expressing his feelings—seem like the worst person in the world.

That's dangerous. Social media posts can quickly lead to cyberbullying, and that can have terrible effects on the people who are on the receiving end. Young men and women have committed suicide after people attacked and shamed them on Instagram, Facebook, or Twitter. Those victims felt there was no way back, that there was no redemption. That's just wrong.

I had a talk with Malik, letting him know that it's fine to feel the way he feels, but he has to learn how to express himself in a way that doesn't hurt black women or anyone else. That was the way for the situation to be handled, and I think Malik has learned from that.

We shouldn't rush to judgment. And when people say that they're sorry, we should be willing to accept it, to be more sympathetic and forgiving.

For someone who does something horrific, like hurting a child, the road to redemption is long, maybe even endless. But you shouldn't judge a man or woman in their forties for a stupid mistake they made in their twenties. Look at the all the years in between. What have they done? What have they said? What is redeeming?

And if each of us wants to be forgiven in turn, we have to learn to say that we're sorry. If we have done something wrong, we need to look at how to make it right. If we want people to extend their arms to us, we have to extend our arms to them. We have to make amends, and learn to love and forgive ourselves, too.

STAND FOR SOMETHING

The day that I gave my life to Jesus Christ was also the same day that I joined the NAACP. I was eight years old.

That's the way it was at New Mt. Olive Baptist Church, a sanctuary presided over by the legendary Reverend Edward Gardner. That's the way it was in my hometown, the cradle of the civil rights movement: Birmingham, Alabama.

Before we were baptized, we were given applications to fill out—to join not only the historic, nearly century-old National Association for the Advancement of Colored People, but also the Southern Christian Leadership Conference, which had been cofounded by the Reverend Dr. Martin Luther King Jr. in January 1957.

Basically, when we were pledging our love and allegiance to a higher power, we were also pledging our commitment to civil rights and social justice. That was Birmingham. The struggle was in the air and in our blood. The struggle was real.

You have to stand up for others, whether it's the kid on the playground who's being bullied, the young black men being murdered by police when they've done nothing wrong, or the poor and sick whose safety nets seem always on the brink of being ripped out from beneath their feet.

I'd rather be dead with nothing and have stood for something than have all the riches in the world and have not stood for anything. I may spin hip-hop, make prank calls, and crack out jokes, but the most important thing I do when I sit down in front of a microphone is to try to fight for the people who don't have a voice.

I've used my mic to speak to the kids who are trapped in a bad school system. I have used my voice to get people elected to the school board who might bring about change. I used my fame to call attention to a girl being mistreated by a system that too often fails to recognize the humanity of young people of color.

And I used my mic to introduce my listeners to a young black senator with an African name who wanted to be president. I used the platform God gave me to spread the word that what seems impossible is still worth fighting for. You have to stand for something.

———————

AT THE TIME that I was baptized, I'm not sure I understood the magnitude of the civil rights struggle. I always attended integrated schools. And even though I heard the N-word every now and then—including one time from a kid named Bobby Johnson, whom I beat within an inch of his life for saying it—by the 1970s, bigotry wasn't usually blatant or constant, even in Birmingham.

Still, one of the warriors who had fought to make things better was standing in front of me every Sunday. His name was Edward Gardner.

The Reverend Edward Gardner was a lion in the civil rights movement who led our church for more than fifty years. He had been one of Dr. Martin Luther King Jr.'s soldiers. In his pastor's study, there was a picture of him sitting with the great man, Dr. King himself. I remember gazing at that photograph when I got older and thinking that I couldn't believe I knew someone who had known Dr. King.

Reverend Gardner let you know in his fiery sermons that the Bible was a living, breathing thing. When it talked about right and wrong, courage and brotherhood, those weren't just bromides or fables from a long-ago time. Those were words to live by, instructions to follow today.

Birmingham is a town that's known around the world for what happened there during the civil rights movement. In the fight for black people to have the same rights as every other American—to be able to sit where they liked when they wanted to rest, to take a front seat on a bus that their taxes paid for, to cast a vote for the politicians who would govern their lives—African-Americans faced threats of violence and death every day.

There were so many explosions, people started calling the city Bombingham. One of those bombs killed four precious schoolgirls—Denise McNair, Cynthia Wesley, Addie Mae Collins, and Carole Robertson—who were simply worshipping at 16th Street Baptist Church one Sunday in September 1963. There was no justice. There was no peace.

And then there was Bull Connor, Birmingham's infamous "commissioner of public safety." He was so hell-bent on fighting integration that he turned police dogs and fire hoses on boys and girls. Those black and white images of Birmingham are framed forever, for the world to see.

So, black folks in Birmingham were ever vigilant. Always front and center in our minds was the need to fight for justice.

Every one of my relatives had a picture of Dr. King hanging on a wall, to the point that when I was really young and didn't know who he was yet, I assumed that he was a long-dead uncle.

I remember that my grandmother's friend Margaret Phillips, whom we all called Aunt Beulah, had one of those creepy velvet portraits of Dr. King tacked up in a bedroom. You know the kind that absorbed the light, so that when you flipped the switch off, the eyes still glowed and seemed to be staring at you in the dark? It was one of those.

Sometimes, when Grandmama Ada and I would visit Aunt Beulah, we would spend the night. I would be scared to death looking at that painting, or rather watching that painting look at me. I would put my head under the blankets and nuzzle up in the crook of my grandmother's arm. Man, I couldn't wait for morning to come.

My grandmother Ada also had pictures of President John F. Kennedy and his brother Robert sitting side by side in her living room. At first, as with Dr. King, I didn't exactly know who they were. But I did think they looked familiar.

Finally, I figured it out. Those were the white dudes who sold insurance to my grandmother. I wasn't sure why that merited their pictures being set next to the photograph of my long-dead uncle Martin, but I figured Grandmama Ada had her reasons.

Back at my family's apartment, my mother displayed pictures of the great orator and activist Malcolm X, as well as Dr. King. Consciousness permeated our home. It was there in the snippets of conversation I overheard my mother and her friends having about local and national politics. It was there in the music of Marvin Gaye, spinning on my mother's stereo, asking what in the world was going on.

You'd walk through the neighborhood, and along with good old-fashioned funk, there was message music blasting through car windows. The O'Jays said you've got to give the people what they want. George Clinton said that with the rhythm it took to dance to what we had to live through, we could dance underwater and not get wet.

He had that right. I started to understand.

By the time I finished elementary school, if I thought black kids were getting hassled more in a classroom than their white peers, I would question the teacher. I watched the television news and tried to keep up with what was happening in our city and in our state.

But I was twelve years old when all the history, all the talk of responsibility and struggle, really hit home. It was June 22, 1979, the day that Bonita Carter got killed.

Carter was sitting in her car when she was shot to death by a cop named George Sands. A local store had been robbed, and the officer wrongly went after Carter, who he thought played a role in the crime. Carter was only twenty years old. Sands was not charged with anything for what he had done, and he even had the backing of Birmingham's mayor, David Vann. But black Birmingham took to the streets.

Our protests made national news. I was one of the thousands of people out there marching and protesting. My anger was personal. Mr. and Mrs. Carter, Bonita's parents, lived around the corner from my grandmother Ada. They had been friends of our family. It broke my heart to see them, grieving but still trying to be strong, on the television every night.

I remember the civil rights activists and icons Jesse Jackson and Joseph Lowery coming to town. I remember riding the bus with my mother to take our demands for justice to the steps of city hall. Unfortunately, they never did punish that police officer. But David Vann didn't win another term in office, either. We didn't get all that we wanted, but Birmingham had stood for something. Ordinary people had once again cast a light on a terrible wrong and gained a small victory.

Nowadays, I often think of Bonita Carter. It's heartbreaking that nearly forty years later, we are still waking up in the morning, flipping on the television, and hearing about an innocent black person being gunned down by a police officer or vigilante who goes scot-free. It's getting harder as an American to believe all this talk about freedom and democracy

Trayvon Martin. Michael Brown. Philando Castile. Jordan Davis. Tamir Rice. The list of names is dizzying. The crimes and injustice are disgusting. As a black man, I have to tell you that it's also terrifying.

All of this unpunished violence leaves you walking on eggshells. It makes you suspicious of others sometimes, assuming the worst about their actions or intentions.

Because I am black, does that stranger think I'm a lesser person without knowing whom I've loved, what I've done, or who I am? Did that salesperson place the change on the counter instead of in my hand because she did not want to touch me? Why did that Uber driver pull up, see me, and suddenly mention another prebooked trip that he had to make?

I'm not saying that those questions never crossed my mind before now, but these days, they pop into my mind a lot more often.

A few months ago, I was driving to the airport. I had to fly to St. Louis to do a live broadcast for the radio show. Suddenly, lights started flashing in my rearview mirror. It was about two or three in the morning.

I will not beat around the bush. I was a nervous wreck. I heard the officer slam the police cruiser's door, and as he walked toward me, those colored lights blinking in the background, all I could think of was my kids.

You have to know what you need to do to get through encounters with police. It's something that every black person, particularly black boys and men, has to learn. It's critical, so that they can get back home to their kids, so that they can get back home to their families, so that they can survive.

I started shaking.

"Oh Lord," I thought. "I've got to make it back home."

"Hello, officer," I started saying through my open window. "I'm Rickey Smiley. I've got a radio show and I'm just heading to the airport to perform out of town . . ."

He stopped me. He sensed my fear. He could see it. Instead of exploiting it, he made an effort to calm me down. That policeman turned out to be a good dude.

"Sir," he said. "Relax. Your tag is expired, I just need to see your license and your registration."

Ultimately, he gave me a warning and let me drive away. That cop was one of the good ones, but he might not have been. My tag had expired, so he had a legitimate reason to stop me. But if he had been one of those officers who profile and harass some motorists because of the color of their skin, it would have been crazy for me to take a stand with him at two thirty in the morning, to have protested or gotten belligerent with no witnesses in sight.

You have to know when to take a stand and when to stand down. Civil rights workers were drilled on how to respond to different situations, on how to act in the short term in order to get long-term gains. That kind of discipline, that kind of understanding, is still necessary today, in all aspects of our lives.

I was determined to be as cooperative as possible. If he abused his power and I was able to get out of there alive, I could get a lawyer and come after him later. But in the moment, I needed to be sensible. Sometimes cooperation is not enough, like in the case of Philando Castile, who was completely cooperative with the officers and got shot anyway. But you have to try. It's a shame that that's the way you have to think in the twenty-first century. But that's the way it is—for now.

Still, we all have to remember that each of us has the power to change things. In a moment that could wind up being a matter of life and death, we have to use common sense. Later, you can bring to light what occurred. You can hire an attorney. You can lodge a formal complaint. You can rally your neighbors or lead a march through the streets.

And you can challenge the injustices that you might encounter on any given day. Don't let a salesperson mistreat you when your purchase is helping to pay their commission. If you hand that salesperson your credit card, and they put it on the counter instead of in your palm, you let them know to give that card back to you the way that you gave it to them. If the bad attitude continues, take the matter to their supervisor.

If a teacher is treating your child unfairly, go to the principal and, if you have to, the school board. If a waiter is being rude, you should not only skip the tip, but also ask to speak to the manager or owner. Demand to be treated with respect.

———————

I'M NOT CRAZY about flying, but given my career, I often have no other choice than to get on a plane. Since the late 1990s, when my career really accelerated, I have always flown first class.

Often, the flight attendants are gracious, particularly since I go out of my way to treat with kindness people who are working hard— stowing bags, handing out drinks, answering passengers' questions. But as an African-American man who's also usually casually dressed when I'm flying, so I can be comfortable and relax before a show, there have been occasions when I definitely had to set a flight attendant straight.

One time, as soon as I boarded a flight, I could tell this particular flight attendant was going to be trouble. She looked me up and down and clearly didn't think I belonged in the front of the plane.

After everybody was seated, she made a beeline for me, asking to see my ticket.

I asked her why she needed to see my ticket when she had a list with the name of every passenger in that cabin, as well as the seat that they were assigned. Clearly, and loudly, I let her know that she could see my ticket after she asked to see the ticket of every white passenger sitting around me.

Her face turned red. But I wasn't finished.

"Let me guess," I began. "Your best friend is black. The tires on your car are black. You use black hair dye. So there's no way you can be prejudiced."

Those words shut her down. When she finally backed away and went to the galley in the front of the plane, I could see her wiping tears from her eyes. But I wasn't moved. Out of her own ignorance, she tried to humiliate me, and I wasn't going to tolerate it. Dr. King and countless others fought and died so that I could sit in the seat I paid for and not be treated like a second-class citizen. So I stood firm. You're not going to get away with trying to mistreat me.

That flight attendant didn't know that I was a child of the movement. She didn't know that I was a son of Birmingham. She also didn't know that she was dealing with a comedian. I've been handling hecklers for twenty-five years, so I'm quick. I'll embarrass you in a minute and won't feel bad for a second about doing it.

Another time, I needed to take on a fellow passenger. I was flying to Charleston, South Carolina. I'd been up since early that morning, doing my radio show, and I needed to get a little rest before I performed that evening. I was sitting next to the window in the first row, and I pushed the button to lean back my seat so I could fall asleep.

But something was blocking me. I thought the seat might have been broken, but when I turned around, there was a white man who had propped his leg in such a way that I couldn't recline. "My leg is right here," he said coldly.

I took my seat belt off, slid out of my row, and stood at the end of his. I leaned over that man's seatmate and put my finger in his face.

"I'm not asking you," I said quietly, "I'm telling you. I'm pushing my seat back, and you're going to move your leg so that I can do it. Do you understand me?"

A flight attendant hurried over, asking if we had a problem. I looked at him. "Do we?"

"No," he said. "We don't have a problem."

When I took my seat and pushed the button again, that seat reclined just fine. But by that time, I was so angry, I couldn't even doze off. I'll admit that many people have far worse problems than a jerk sitting behind them in first class. But I was mad, and this guy's bad attitude was infecting me like poison.

Then the man sitting beside me, who also happened to be white, put his hand on my wrist and squeezed it. I thought to myself, "Am I going to have to fight somebody today?"

I don't know what my seatmate's political affiliation was, what he did for a living, or where he lived. But he knew what had just happened wasn't right. He looked me in the eye.

"I just want to apologize to you, sir," he said quietly.

I told him that he didn't have to apologize for someone else, and I knew that not everybody was like that man behind me. But thanks.

When the plane landed in Charleston and we prepared to disembark, the tension was so thick and the cabin was so quiet that you could have heard a mouse pee on a cotton ball.

Since I was at the very front, I was one of the first at the door. Before it opened, I felt a tap on my shoulder.

"Oh my God," I thought. "Let me be calm, so I don't do something that gets me on the no-fly list."

I turned around. It was the guy who'd tried to block my seat from reclining.

"Sir," he said, with a deep Southern drawl, "I'd like to apologize from the bottom of my heart and the pit of my soul."

I looked at him for a second. "Sir," I began, "we're all heading somewhere, trying to take care of business. We have to treat each other with respect. I'm still mad, but I accept your apology."

I didn't make my response about race or racism. For all I knew the guy was just an entitled jerk rather than a bigot. But either way, I focused on its being a matter of right and wrong, of simple, common courtesy. This was a public space that we all shared, and no one person's needs or feelings superseded anyone else's. I left it to him to reflect more deeply on what he had done and why he had done it.

Still, I want to take a moment here to make another important point. Yes, there are bad people in the world. Yes, there are hateful people in the world. And sadly, we're living in a particular moment when some people feel emboldened to loudly proclaim their intolerance and even act on it.

But there are plenty of good people, too. I remember on that flight when the flight attendant asked to see my ticket, another passenger, a white man sitting beside me, apologized for her outrageous behavior. He knew right from wrong, just like my seatmate on that flight to Charleston.

The cop who pulled me over when I was driving to the airport was a young white man who recognized that I was nervous and made an effort to make me feel comfortable, to ease my mind. When you have a run-in with someone who is biased, who is hateful, it can cloud your perception of an entire group, it can darken your perception of the world, and it can make you see prejudice even in instances when it might not exist. But there couldn't be bad if there wasn't also good.

There were white people who marched and died in the civil rights movement. There are people out there of all ethnicities and religious faiths who are advocating for equality and fighting for justice.

To make sure that we leave behind a better world than the one we were born into, each of us has a part to play. We can make a difference, using whatever platforms we have at our disposal. We can issue a call for action on Facebook. We can spread a little knowledge on Twitter.

Your church committee is a platform. Your high school glee club is a platform. Your sorority is a platform. You can even start to move the wheels of change all by yourself.

———————

WHEN I MOVED to Dallas, Texas, to launch *The Rickey Smiley Morning Show*, I felt like God had given me a tremendous gift. I was no longer the sidekick. I had top billing and a lot more control.

I felt that with opportunity came great responsibility. The music and the humor were vehicles to get people to listen. They were a way to grab folks' attention. Then, when I had it, I could shine a spotlight on issues happening in the community.

I jumped in with both feet. I went to city council meetings and met with county commissioners. I invited community leaders—activists, doctors, businesspeople—on my show. And I protested the unjust treatment of fourteen-year-old Shaquanda Cotton.

Helping to get that young woman released from jail was a major victory. Another was helping to get Craig Watkins elected district attorney.

I invoked the spirit of Rosa Parks, the mother of the civil rights movement, as well as slain civil rights activist Medgar Evers, and nearly every other civil rights icon that I could think of, to encourage my listeners to vote for Craig Watkins. He is an acclaimed lawyer with lots of ideas for how to bring fairness to the so-called justice system. He was trying to become the first black district attorney ever elected in Dallas County.

I invited him to appear on my show, and I hit the campaign trail with him, reminding my listeners and anyone else I ran into to head to the polls. When all the ballots were finally counted on Election Day in November 2006, Watkins had not only made history in Dallas County but was also the first black district attorney ever elected in the state of Texas.

If you want to spark change, you have to be willing to take the first step. There are a whole lot of black judges who got elected or appointed to the bench because *The Rickey Smiley Morning Show* spent time educating the public about their candidacies and spurring people to vote.

Then, not long after Craig Watkins became district attorney, I did my small part in helping a man running for the ultimate political prize: the presidency of the United States.

I cohosted a small fund-raiser for Barack Obama at a friend's home. Dallas was one of Obama's stops after he'd announced in Illinois that he was going to make a bid for the White House. I remember how he jumped out of a car, surrounded by members of the Secret Service. I shook his hand for the first time, and we hit it off right away. There were only about thirty of us at that backyard gathering, and Obama and I spent a lot of time kidding around, talking, and snapping pictures. He was incredibly down-to-earth. I not only respected what he was trying to achieve; I also liked him as a person.

After Obama won the presidency, I went on to work with him and his administration, which was trying to empower young men of color with the initiative My Brother's Keeper. One time, I went to the White House for a meeting but was delayed by security because of a glitch with my identification. When I walked in, I tried to quietly slide into my seat, since I was late and the meeting had already started.

But anybody who's ever seen the annual White House Correspondents' Dinner on C-SPAN knows that Barack Obama is a funny dude.

"Ladies and gentlemen," he said with that unmistakable cadence, "here is Rickey Smiley, arriving late to a meeting with the president of the United States. Thanks for joining us, Rickey."

I was so embarrassed. But it was all in good fun, and I cracked up laughing like everybody else.

I remember another time when I attended a concert at the White House. The Obamas were gracious hosts who really made that grand manor the people's house, filling it with artists and musicians, from Lin Manuel Miranda, creator of the groundbreaking play *Hamilton*, to the conscious rapper Common. This one particular evening, Aretha Franklin, the queen of soul, was among the legends who were performing.

It was like she had caught the Holy Ghost. She was singing her heart out. We sat in our seats, shoulders shimmying, heads nodding, hips shifting, enjoying the music. Aretha dropped to her knees.

"Help me up," she sang.

"Help me up!" the man next to her onstage crooned.

"Help me up," the queen sang again.

"Help me up!" the other vocalist wailed. Man, they were getting into a call-and-response groove!

Finally, Aretha stopped singing and made it plain. "I can't get up.

Help me!" She had gotten down on the ground, and now she couldn't get back on her feet.

When the audience realized what was going on, it seemed like everybody in the room turned around to look at me. It was like they needed the comedian in the room to give them permission to laugh.

The president, sitting in the front row, turned slightly in his chair and looked at me out of the corner of his eye. I could read his body language. "Don't do it, Rickey," his look said.

It took every ounce of strength for me not to fall out of my chair howling, like I used to do when I was a kid in Miss Avery's classroom. But I held it together—at least until after the concert.

Everyone was chatting and mingling. Michelle Obama, the first lady, walked toward me. Her smile was already twitching. We burst out laughing as we hugged and held each other up. I swear, I think we stood there cracking up for at least five minutes.

I had a lot of fun with the first black president and first lady of the United States.

Having a relationship with such historic figures was just icing on the cake for me. The more important thing was trying to get people motivated to take action, to campaign and vote, so that people of their caliber could get a chance to lead in the first place.

When I got on the air in Dallas, countless people told me that they had never heard a show quite like mine. Now, with my show on the air in roughly eighty markets, I continue to invite people like the motivational speaker Warren Ballentine and the renowned activist Al Sharpton to speak to my listeners.

As a comedian, I am really not doing anything new. Legends like Richard Pryor and the great Dick Gregory constantly used humor like a sword to cut away double-talk, and like a light to expose hypocrisy and injustice.

I'm proud to see a new generation carrying on that tradition. I really love Trevor Noah, the young South African comic who took over *The Daily Show* from Jon Stewart, a truth-teller in his own right. Noah brings his own style to that program, and I think he is brilliant and incisive, as well as just plain funny. He's also surrounded by a great team. I am a mentor to one of the other comics on his show, Roy Wood Jr., who is incredibly talented. He's appeared in various movies and television shows, and I believe he's on his way to becoming a household name.

Even if you don't want to use your art to make a statement, I think it's important that those of us who are blessed with a little celebrity use that extra visibility to help others. It makes me angry when people who get rich off the community—the folks who buy their music, go to their movies, buy their endorsed products—don't give back to that same community in either word or deed.

History is filled with athletes and entertainers who had so much more to lose, but who laid it all on the line to do what they believed was right. The late, great Muhammad Ali wasn't the greatest of all time just because he went toe-to-toe with Joe Frazier or won a historic bout with George Foreman. He's the greatest because of what he did when he wasn't boxing.

He spoke of how he had been unable to eat in a restaurant in his hometown of Louisville, Kentucky, after winning a gold medal for the nation at the Rome Olympic Games in 1960. He was stripped of his livelihood for refusing to fight in Vietnam. When he had to endure racism in his own country virtually every day, he didn't see the sense in attacking people who had never done a thing to him.

There were others in the spotlight who took a stand, sometimes at great peril—basketball great Kareem Abdul-Jabbar, football phenomenon Jim Brown, and actor Harry Belafonte. And there are celebrities today who are also taking action, whether it's quarterback Colin Kaepernick, kneeling to protest social injustice, or Cleveland Cavalier LeBron James, who, after someone scrawled a racial epithet on his home, linked his hurt with those far less famous when he said it's still hard to be black in America. If you're fortunate enough to be well-known, use your bullhorn to speak for the voiceless, use your status to start a conversation.

A lot of people have told me that they weren't into politics before they started listening to my morning show. I've been able to bring people to the polls through hip-hop. I've been able to bring people closer to God through music and laughter. We all need a respite sometimes, to relax and just drift away in a song or some jokes. But other times, we have to get educated and take action, too.

And even when people don't seem to be listening, when they say things like their votes won't make a difference or certain things in society will never change, you can't give up. If we all stopped talking, teaching, and fighting, where would our communities, our cities, and our country be?

To make a difference, you don't have to be an extraordinary individual like Nelson Mandela, who spent decades in prison only to forgive his captors, or Medgar Evers and Dr. King, who sacrificed their lives. You don't have to be rich to bring about change or be a celebrity to exercise power.

If you feel your neighborhood needs a community center, if you think that there aren't enough activities for the youth, if you believe that a local lawmaker cares more about power than the people, you can send an email or organize a fund-raiser. You can canvass door-to-door or run for office yourself.

You just have to be willing and motivated. You just have to stand for something.

PASS THE BATON

I f I needed to sit and jot down the name of every person who has helped me in my life, I would run out of paper, pencils, and pens before I was anywhere near finished.

I had multiple generations—parents, uncles, grandparents, even great-grandparents—feeding me wisdom and love. Then there were all the other mothers and fathers who surrounded me.

There were folks like Charles and Brenda Lockhart, who lived across the street from Mattie and Ernest, my father's parents. There was Mr. Gregg Turner, who would take me and his son, Kermit, to football practice, when we played on the Tarrant Wildcats peewee team. And Earnest and Gertrude Thompson were another set of elders who lived nearby.

I grew up in each of their houses. Their children were like my brothers and sisters. They all looked out for me.

The Lockharts kept me on my toes academically. Mr. Lockhart was a middle school principal and Mrs. Lockhart was a school counselor, so when it came to grades or manners, they didn't play. I remember that Mrs. Lockhart, who spoke very proper English, wouldn't even let us kids say the word "lie." She said that it didn't sound right, that it was the three-letter equivalent of a four-letter word. Now I don't allow my own kids to say it. I prefer that they say that someone simply isn't telling the truth. And when "lie" occasionally slips out of my mouth today, I whip my neck around to see if Mrs. Lockhart is standing nearby, even when I'm a thousand miles away from Birmingham.

It was great that my sister, Karon, and I had all these brothers and sisters to hang out with. There were Chuck, Jason, and Jarrod Lockhart, who were all scholars. They encouraged me to do better in school by their example. Then there were all the Thompson kids, Mott, Melvin, Cookie, Chris, Chandra, Tiny, and Earnest Jr.

We'd spend the night with one another, talking in the dark when we were supposed to be asleep. We'd meet up at recess to play tag or talk junk. We'd hit a baseball in the backyard or crack jokes during Sunday school. It was a whole lot of fun.

It was also nice that any night of the week, I could go to one of their homes and eat dinner. Mrs. Lockhart and Mrs. Thompson would cook tasty, All-American Southern suppers. I'm talking English peas and cube steak, pork chops and mashed potatoes. In contrast, my grandmothers' cooking choices could be challenging. Mattie and Ada liked to make chitterlings, pig ears, fatback, and pig feet. I don't think there was one part of the hog that didn't end up in their ovens at some point.

There was no end to the exotic foods bubbling in my grandmothers' kitchens. I'd come home from school and the house would be smelling good. My mouth would be watering, my stomach would be rumbling, and I'd head right to the stove. Then, when I slid the lid off of the pot, do you know what would be staring back at me? Some chicken feet.

Or my grandmothers might be boiling pots of butter beans and squash, with some slimy okra lurking in the middle. We were supposed to choke that down with slabs of corn bread.

Every now and then, my uncle Jessie would bring over some deer meat, which wasn't too bad. It was like chomping on some tough steak. But possibly the worst thing I ever ate was this concoction my grandmother Ada would sometimes cook called white meat.

I'm not sure whether it was bacon, fat, tripe, or some combination of all of the above, but she'd bake it in the oven. When it finally landed on your dinner plate, you'd take a bite and have to chew it for days. Truly. I could go to bed with that white meat in my mouth, grind my teeth all night long, and by morning it still wasn't digestible. It was terrible. So I loved going to the neighbors' to eat.

But beyond the good home cooking, the real blessing was having this wide circle that held me in its embrace, whether it was welcoming me to their dinner tables, checking on my report cards, or taking me out to play football at the park.

Some of us are more fortunate than others when it comes to friends, family, and mentors. But every single one of us has someone who did something to push us along our life path, and each of us has some talent, gift, or good fortune that we can pass along to someone else.

I have fans whose appreciation of my prank calls, characters, and jokes has enabled me to have an amazing career. There are countless comedians, from Steve Harvey to Cedric the Entertainer to Earthquake, who have always encouraged me. There was the kind but stern police officer I met at a McDonald's when I was in high school, who pulled me up in order to set me straight, and Tim McReynolds, the dapper sales manager at 95.7 who taught me not to accept more favors than I was comfortable paying back.

There is no way with all of the advice, love, and support that I've been given that I could refuse to offer even a little bit to someone else. It's important to pass the baton, to lift up someone coming behind you.

Those people who pull up the ladder once they've gotten to the top floor are not only being selfish, but they may also leave themselves stranded when they need a helping hand.

THE FIRST TIME I appeared on *Showtime at the Apollo*, the comedian Mark Curry was the host.

I had met Mark briefly before when he'd performed in Birmingham, but mostly I was just a big fan. He had a look and a style when he performed that made you feel like you were watching your cool buddy from around the corner crack jokes—and your buddy just happened to be funnier than any professional on television. Mark just had an easy, warm, relatable way about him.

My grandmother Mattie loved Mark Curry, too. When he became *Showtime*'s emcee, she and I would be sure to watch every weekend. The only problem was that she kept thinking he was the R & B balladeer Freddie Jackson.

"I didn't know Freddie Jackson did comedy," Grandma Mattie would say.

"Grandmama, that is Mark Curry, *not* Freddie Jackson," I'd reply.

She'd been mixing up Mark and Freddie, who both had round brown faces but certainly weren't twins, since Mark got his own sitcom, *Hangin' with Mr. Cooper*, in the early 1990s.

"Freddie Jackson has a new TV show," she told me excitedly.

"Grandmama," I said patiently, "Freddie Jackson doesn't tell jokes, and Mark Curry isn't going around singing 'You Are My Lady.'"

"Oh," she'd say, a little embarrassed. "I keep getting everything crossed up."

Obviously, my getting a chance to perform at the Apollo that first time in the late 1990s was a big deal. But I was a little paranoid.

Even though I'd been in front of hundreds of live audiences by that point, the Apollo was a whole different ball game. It was a legendary venue, the show was watched by a national audience, and that crowd was about as rough and rowdy a bunch as you could find.

I basically sneaked away from Birmingham to do the taping. That way, if things didn't go well and my routine didn't air, no one would be the wiser.

I was right to be worried. The day of the taping, as soon as Mark introduced me and said that I was from Birmingham, that New York crowd started to boo. But Mark did something I'll always appreciate.

"Look," he said, whispering in my ear. "Don't pay any attention to them. Just play to the camera, because your stuff is going to air."

I needed to hear that, because my first impulse was just to give up and walk back off the stage. The crowd laughed a little bit here and there, but mostly they booed their behinds off. I got through my three-minute routine and got the hell out. When I went back to Birmingham, I didn't tell anybody about that appearance. I hoped everybody would be out to dinner at Dreamland Bar-B-Que that night and wouldn't see that I had gone to New York and bombed. That was going to be one evening that Grandmama Mattie and I didn't catch *Showtime*.

So I was at home, cooling my heels to some classic rock, when my phone started blowing up.

"How come you didn't tell me you were going to be on the *Apollo*?" one of my buddies yelled excitedly when I picked up.

A few minutes later, *brrrrinnnnggg!*

"How could you appear on the *Apollo* and not let us know? We could have had a party and watched it all together at my house," another friend said.

"Oh, I was just being modest," I lied.

"Well you killed it, man," he continued. "The crowd was loving you. Congratulations!"

What the . . . ? I was confused.

As it turned out, the producers had shown my routine, but they edited out the audience that booed me and showed another group laughing hysterically at some other comedian instead. That's the way taped television goes sometimes. I was thankful.

But even more than those producers and editors, I appreciated Mark Curry for calming me down. It was enough so that I could go on with the show and not blow a big moment. I have experienced that kind of support throughout my career, whether it was Mark encouraging me to ignore the crowd, or Cedric the Entertainer giving a name to my most famous character, Lil Darryl, or Steve Harvey recommending me for the opportunity of a lifetime when he brought me to Dallas and helped me launch my own radio show.

Mark Curry, Tommy Davidson, Steve Harvey, and Cedric the Entertainer were just a few of the dudes who really set off black comedy in the 1990s. And each of them, plus many more, looked out for me. So I've tried to do the same, helping up-and-coming comics kick-start their careers.

I've taken some very talented young men and women on the road for the first time. I've pulled together tours so they could polish their timing and get exposure to a wider audience. I've tried to be a big brother and friend whom they can talk to, question, and create with.

I first met Corey Holcomb when I was in his hometown of Chicago. Corey was just starting out, doing open mic nights, like I had done back at the Comedy Club in Birmingham. He introduced himself to me one day and said that he wanted to move beyond Chicago. He was eager, he was ambitious, and he was funny, so I said, let's go on the road.

I started having him open for me at some of my shows. He'd come to Birmingham, we'd hop in my car, and we'd head to an appearance.

I remember one day we were rolling through South Carolina when we almost got into a fistfight—over some doughnuts. He was screaming at the top of his lungs that Dunkin' Donuts was better than Krispy Kreme.

Now, being that I'm from Alabama, that was sheer blasphemy. Krispy Kreme is practically the state's official dessert. So I asked Corey if he was out of his mind. They didn't have Dunkin' Donuts where I lived, but I didn't have to taste one to know that there was no way on earth they could be more delicious than those sweet, gooey Krispy Kremes.

Then Corey had the nerve to say that he had never tasted a Krispy Kreme. I thought, "This dude has been sheltered and deprived." I said that if he said one more word about some doughnut holes from Dunkin' being better than those Krispy treats, I was putting his butt out of my car and he could walk back to Chicago.

We were driving through Columbia, South Carolina, when I made a detour off the highway. Then I saw it, a Krispy Kreme sign beckoning me like that spaceship in the movie *Close Encounters of the Third Kind*. And it had the hot light on—that meant a fresh batch of doughnuts was coming straight out of the fryer!

I stopped and bought a dozen. When I opened the box up in the car, they were so warm that the steam fogged up the windows. Corey's face had the look of defeat before he even took his first bite.

He reached in that box, plucked out a pastry, and for the next few hours, he didn't even make eye contact with me. Silently, he gazed out of the passenger window all the way back to Birmingham. The only time he opened his mouth was to eat another Krispy Kreme.

Today, Corey's career is on fire. His stories about the good, the bad, and the ugly in relationships have earned him fans all over the country. He's hosted his own specials, appeared on popular television shows like *Everybody Hates Chris*, and even voiced a cartoon character named Robert Tubbs on *The Cleveland Show*.

Corey's often been my guest on the radio. He's thanked me for giving him an opportunity, but I don't feel like I did anything special. He was going to shine regardless. I just brought him into the spotlight a little more quickly. And it was the least that I could do, given all that has been done for me.

Another one of my protégés is Roy Wood Jr. We've walked in the same footsteps. He is also from Birmingham, and he worked at 95.7, my radio alma mater, for years as a writer and producer. He's proudly carried on the prank call tradition, and he was one of the top contenders on *Last Comic Standing*, a show that featured up-and-coming comics on NBC.

Then, two years ago, Roy got the break of a lifetime when he became a correspondent on *The Daily Show*. One day soon, I'm going to just hop on a plane and surprise him at one of his performances. I'm so proud of what he's accomplished. That's the way I feel about so many of these young guys whom I've helped mentor and who've gone on to do big things.

And don't think that I only look out for male comics. Some of the funniest comedians in the business—Mo'Nique, Leslie Jones, Sommore—are women. And I think the next big star is Rita Brent, a young lady from Jackson, Mississippi, whom I've also taken under my wing.

Bruce Ayers, the owner of the Comedy Club in Birmingham, who introduced me to Steve Harvey, is the one who first connected me with Rita.

"It's time to pay it forward," he told me as I shook Rita's hand. Based on all Bruce had meant to me, I would have volunteered to help

Rita's career without even hearing her tell one joke. But when I did hear her routine, I laughed so hard, I doubled over. She had confidence. She had presence. She had swagger. She has been on the road with me ever since.

Rita is a dream mentee, and in some ways, she reminds me of myself. She also attended a historically black college, Jackson State University; she is a member of the sorority Delta Sigma Theta; she hosts a public radio show in Jackson; and she is a trained musician. I have had her come on my morning show so she can hone her radio chops for a national audience. And when we tour, we talk in between shows about the nuances of timing, flow, and how you have to read the room and zig and zag.

As a comedian you have to be quick on your feet, and Rita is a fast learner. One time, we did a show in Little Rock. Rita is meticulous, so she had written up notes for her routine, but when I warmed up the crowd, I switched my stories to match the feel of the room. I talked a lot about Southern and family life—my aunt who was scared of her own shadow, and those salty Oscar Mayer school snacks that are probably terrible for your blood pressure but that you can't resist because they taste so darn good.

Rita was watching from the wings, and just like that, she flipped her script. She went onstage and talked about church, as well as office bathroom etiquette. That was quite a combination—and she killed it. I believe that she's going to go far in the world of comedy.

That particular show in Arkansas was part of Rickey Smiley and Friends, a tour I do with a rotating bunch of talented comedians, from Junebug to J. B. Smoove to Kelly "K-Dubb" Walker. J. B. and I are close buddies who came up in the business together, but when I perform with some of the younger comedians who are just getting their feet wet, I definitely try to offer advice along with the opportunity.

I tell them not to get distracted partying and clubbing after their shows. In some ways, the joke-telling is the easy part. It's the writing, the rehearsing, the flying, and the driving that can wear you down. We are professionals, not clowns, and we have to be focused, we have to be rested, and we have to be ready.

Each of the men and women I am trying to help has grabbed hold of their breaks and held on tight. They dress well. They show up on time. They work on their craft. Nobody drinks, or hangs out late, or misses flights. They have taken the baton and run with it.

Another person I often appear with on the road is a comic named Special K. He's also one of the cast members on *The Rickey Smiley Morning Show*.

I met Special K years ago, when we shared the same manager, a lady named Denise Howard. Denise launched the careers of a lot of Atlanta comedians, and she was one of those people who was like a den mother, master connector, and business mentor all rolled into one. If a bunch of comics had a show in town, she'd let you save the money you'd otherwise have had to spend on a hotel and just pull out blankets and sleep on her floor. I was so grateful for her hospitality and the hard work she did on behalf of my career that I would scrub her whole house when she left in the morning. Then, when she came back home in the evening, I'd have a pot of chicken and dumplings waiting for her on the stove.

As my career progressed, Special K became an opening act for me, as well as a writer and featured player on my radio show. He's also become a great friend. And we have an agreement that, God forbid anything ever happens to him, I'm first in line to marry his wife—a sweet, beautiful lady who is my not-so-secret crush.

AS MUCH AS I love being able to deliver jokes for a living, in many ways it is just a means to an end for me. It's given me a platform to help the less fortunate. It's given me the income to reach out and do for others who are in need.

One Christmas, during my family's annual tradition of taking gifts to some of the poorer corners of Birmingham, we came upon a scene that broke everybody's heart. It was a grandmother who was raising her grandson by herself. We knocked on the door and walked into a darkened room. Forget a Christmas tree. They didn't even have a table. The little boy was eating from a bowl of cereal on the floor.

Along with some groceries, we had intended to give the little boy a couple of toys—a car, a football, maybe some sweatshirts. But seeing how this child was suffering, how his grandmother was trying her best but struggling, we pulled out five or six more gifts—games, *Star Wars* figurines, whatever we had. We wanted to make that little boy happy; we wanted to let him know that whether or not he believed in Santa Claus, there was love and compassion in the world that was real.

When we got ready to leave, his grandmother walked us to the door. "Thank you," she whispered, taking my hand. "If you hadn't come, he wouldn't have had Christmas."

I tried to hold back my tears until I got to my truck. I held tight to her hand and told her that we would be back.

When my kids and I got to our cars, every single one of us broke down crying. We had seen a lot on those Christmas mornings— children in threadbare clothes, apartments that were cold because they didn't have the money to pay for heat. But that scene, that day, hit us like nothing we'd ever felt before. I meant what I'd said. We would be back.

The next day, our whole family headed to Walmart. We filled our cars with everything that they could hold—sheets, clothing, groceries. And what we couldn't carry, we got delivered—new beds, a kitchen table, chairs. The little boy had a smile on his face that could have lit up a whole block, and his grandmother could barely speak. The tears in her eyes told us all that we needed to know.

My children have been so blessed. They live in extreme comfort, and so do I. We didn't need one more iPad. We didn't need one more big-screen television set. We wouldn't have been able to sleep at night if we hadn't done something for that family.

OF COURSE, WHEN you are in the public eye, you get a lot of requests. I'm pretty discerning, and I'd like to think that I can tell if someone is trying to play me. When they're laying it on thick as molasses. When they yell out to me at an appearance that they're looking for a job. When they're rambling about a community group that they want to launch, though they don't have a plan, a mission statement, or a dime of their own money to put into it.

But there is also a lot of suffering in this world. I wake up in the morning, go on my show, and hear it. I go to bed at night with my listeners on my mind, feeling it.

People write me letters. There was a thirty-six-year-old single mother with five children who was struggling to make ends meet, with no support system to lean on. I don't know what I'd mentioned on the air that day, but it gave her something to hold on to.

"Thank you Rickey Smiley so much for what you said on your show," she wrote. "My two sons are out of control, and every time I turn around, as soon as I think my life is up, I lose everything—my house, my cars, my job. Guess what, Rickey? I'm back at that same stage again. But your words today helped me to understand that it's time to move on and that everybody can do it. I laugh at your jokes, but today, you touched my soul. Thank you so much."

Another listener wrote to me about how the music on my show helped to lift him up on a particularly dark day.

"This morning was different for me," he said. "I was driving to the hospital with a deep sadness. My mother was admitted to the hospital Sunday evening, and the outlook is not looking good. I just needed some words of prayer and encouragement. I listened to the beautiful hymn you played. I cried. I smiled. And I praised God for all he has blessed me with. So, I just wanted to say, thank you for making a difference."

I have had people tell me that they were on the verge of committing suicide, but someone or something—maybe Juicy's contagious laugh, maybe that over-the-top story from Gary with da Tea, maybe a great interview with an inspirational figure like Mary J. Blige—pulled them back, and they didn't do it.

I can't tell you how many coffins I've bought for people who didn't have the money to bury a family member. I can't tell you how many times I've dug out a few bills from my pocket to help someone buy groceries or school clothes. But a couple of years ago, I finally realized that I needed to establish a more official system to streamline requests. I wanted to maximize what I could do for people, not just in Birmingham or Atlanta, but all over the country. The Rickey Smiley Foundation was set up in February 2015. And believe me, it stays busy.

Through the foundation, my team gives a car away for charity at the Magic City Classic, the big football game held every year between Alabama A & M and Alabama State University. Every month, we have something that we call "random acts of kindness," where we select a person or family to receive a gift. It might be new bicycles for the kids or enough cash to pay the rent for the next six months.

We do an annual Christmas toy drive, and we've started an entrepreneurial institute to help young people learn skills that can help them work for a lifetime, without having to worry about being hired by someone else.

And we hold events at senior citizen centers and homes. That's one of my favorite activities. I go in there and start spinning tall tales. The folks love it, and I love them. They remind me so much of my grandmothers, Mattie and Ada; my grandfather Ernest; and all of the other elders who have enriched my life.

In its first year, the foundation gave away cash and items worth about $250,000. And there's a lot more to come.

But you don't have to be wealthy or have your own foundation to give to others. I fed the kids in my apartment complex back when I was baking pizzas and selling shoes for a living.

You don't have to be famous to pass along guidance. If you cut hair to make ends meet, and you teach a young person how to do the same, you've passed along knowledge that may one day feed his family. If you caution a young woman about mistakes that you made when you were young, you may pass along real talk that saves that young lady's life.

Each of us has value. Each of us has wisdom. If you have breath in your body, you can pass something along to a child, to a neighbor, to an elder that can help light their way. You don't need to have a lot, as long as whatever you give comes from your heart.

On my last birthday, I didn't want any presents. I didn't care if I got a card. My gift was waking up to the sun streaming through my bedroom windows. My gift was being alive. There was just one person I wanted to see: Carolita, the woman who gave birth to me. And there was just one thing I wanted to do: head to a local soup kitchen so that she and I could pass out meals to the hungry.

I've decided that I am going to do that on my birthday every year, from now on. What better way to celebrate life than to serve up some of its goodness?

ACKNOWLEDGMENTS

First and foremost, I would like to thank God!

To my mother, Carolita, and my stepdad, Edward "Punkin" Lester: thank you for supporting and encouraging me. I want to thank my sister, Karon Smiley, for her unwavering love and always having my back—you're the greatest sister ever. To all my children, Brandon, D'essence, Malik, and Aaryn: Dad loves you and thanks you.

To my amazing grandparents, Ada Mae Armour and Ernest and Mattie Smiley: you truly have been an inspiration. To my uncles, Bruce, Bruh, Herbert, and Sug: words cannot express the gratitude I feel for how each of you helped me become the man that I am today. Thank you, Porshé, ReeRee, Nicole, Craig, Jurnee, Jade, Joc, Terrell, T. J., Genesis, and all my other nieces and nephews for bringing so much joy to my life.

I want to thank my coauthor, Charisse Jones, for all the hard work she put into helping me tell my story. I appreciate your professionalism, your patience, and our new friendship. Thanks for the laughs on that long ride to Little Rock, where you got to see me throw down onstage for the first time, and our day at Dreamland Bar-B-Que, where we ate until we couldn't move. Get ready for book number two!

Special thanks to Nadine Bishop and Patricia Sanders for holding down the home front while I'm on the road. I couldn't do it without you. Ms. Jannie, thank you, too, for all of your love and laughter.

I have unending gratitude for all the awesome religious denominations that have supported me throughout my life and career—the Baptists, Catholics, and members of Full Gospel Fellowship, Church of God in Christ, African Methodist Episcopal, Christian Methodist Episcopal, and Apostolic. To all who have Jesus on their side, but are running for their lives, I hope you enjoy my story.

A special thanks to the esteemed pastors who have welcomed me into their ministries: The Reverend John King, Pastor Kelvin Bryant, Pastor E. Dewey Smith Jr., Pastor Marcus D. Davidson, and Pastor Frederick D. Haynes III.

I want to give a big shout-out to my best friend, Bishop Joseph W. Walker III, and to those longtime school buddies and neighborhood elders who've become family—Gerald Carter, Roosevelt Powell, Glennon Threatt, Judge Nakita Blocton, Mr. and Mrs. Grimes, Mr. and Mrs. Lockhart, and their children Chuck, Jason, and Jarrod.

To Thomas (Uncle Kid) Smiley and Washington Booker (RIP)—thank you for sharing your knowledge and wisdom with me.

Thanks to all those behind the scenes at Bobbcat Films, Radio One, TV One, and Urban One who make the wheels turn on my radio and TV shows, particularly Roger Bobb, Angi Bones, Cathy Hughes, Alfred Liggins, Tim Davies, Marty Raab, who is always there, and David Kantor, who shows incredible patience with me but understands me, which I appreciate more than he knows. In regards to this book, a special shout-out to two ladies who work especially hard with our affiliate radio stations and rallied them around my book tour, Marcella Turk and Melody Talkington, who (along with Junius Thomas) pulled together an amazing tour, and I am eternally grateful for their dedication in promoting this book.

bunker. Craig was a little boy at the time, but in the years since, he'd often heard what happened to Brandon, and so Craig should have learned everything that he needed to know about my detective skills and the types of punishment that I might hand out.

When Brandon threw his little not-so-secret bash, I'd gone out of town to do a show. By that time, Brandon was seventeen years old, so while the younger kids stayed with their mothers, I gave Brandon the chance to stay home by himself. I flew back to Birmingham the next morning, and as soon as I walked into the house, I could tell something wasn't right.

First, I saw footprints in the pale gray carpet. Then, when I looked more closely, I saw a big circle and a smaller circle, so I knew that meant somebody had been in the house wearing high heels.

That couldn't have been D'essence or Aaryn. I didn't allow either one of them to wear heels until the twelfth grade. When D'essence was fifteen and I found a pair of pumps in her closet, I grabbed those skinny-strapped velvet shoes and dumped them right in the trash. So D'essence and Aaryn knew better than to put on some heels, especially inside my house.

There were other telltale signs, like chairs that weren't in the right place and some water marks where cups had been placed on the dining and living room tables without coasters. I know my house like the back of my hand, and Brandon never does a good job cleaning up after himself. He was completely busted.

The clincher was that even if I hadn't seen the evidence firsthand, I would have found out about the party anyway. Brandon's brilliant buddies had posted a whole bunch of pictures on Facebook showing them hoisting their red plastic cups and grinning like they were having the time of their lives—in my house. Some of my friends saw the posts and they couldn't wait to ring my phone and tell me.